TWELVE ROLES OF FACILITATORS

for School Change

R. BRUCE WILLIAMS

SkyLight
Professional Development

Arlington Heights, Illinois

Twelve Roles of Facilitators for School Change

Published by SkyLight Professional Development
2626 S. Clearbrook Dr., Arlington Heights, IL 60005-5310
800-348-4474 or 847-290-6600
Fax 847-290-6609
info@iriskylight.com
http://www.iriskylight.com

Creative Director: Robin Fogarty
Editors: Heidi Ray, Amy Kinsman
Proofreader: Amy Kinsman
Graphic Designer: Heidi Ray
Cover and Illustration Designer: David Stockman
Production Supervisor: Bob Crump

LCCCN 97-70567
ISBN 1-57517-027-2

1951V
Item Number 1490
Z Y X W V U T S R Q P O N M L K J I H G F E
06 05 04 03 02 01 00   15 14 13 12 11 10 9 8 7 6 5

Contents

IRI/SkyLight Training and Publishing, Inc.

Foreword

Human beings have a passion for certainty. We tend to avoid chaos, ambiguity, risk, uncertainty, and change. Instead, we feel secure with stability, cling to tradition, and migrate toward that which is familiar.

Unfortunately (or fortunately, depending on one's perspective), change is ever with us, and it invades our lives with ever-increasing rapidity. Not only is the pace of personal change quickening, but organizational change also is occurring at a faster rate. We have entered a world in which data accumulation doubles in just a matter of years. One projection has been made: By the year 2020, data accumulation will double in just a matter of months, even weeks. The ability of both individuals and organizations to adapt to rapidly changing conditions will be of increasingly critical importance in the years, months, weeks, and days ahead.

While we endure change, we seldom welcome it. Yet our attitude is governed not so much by a dislike of change as by a distaste of *being changed*. We are much more amenable to evolutionary change than to revolutionary upheaval. To avert the pressures of revolutionary transformation, we need to have a well-guided process of change in place, especially in terms of institutional change and, for our purposes here, school change. Guiding the change process requires attention to developing a repertoire of effective strategies that bring participants into the process and lead them

to claim a stake in it, to make a commitment to it, and to share in the leadership of it.

This book shows leaders of the educational change process how to develop the flexibility, openness, and trust needed to make change as painless and as effective as possible. By acquiring the skills of the facilitator, leaders of the change process will know how to navigate uncharted pathways, develop the required skills of their fellow participants, communicate openly and honestly, seek consensus, make intelligent decisions, and solve problems amidst the dynamics of the change process itself and among the many different constituencies that are parties to this process. Facilitation as it is described herein involves locating and developing resources, demands overcoming obstacles and celebrating accomplishments, and requires maintaining faith in the process and the people involved. Facilitation means fostering patience, persistence, and perseverance in the unending, cyclical change process from initiation and development through implementation and evaluation. This is no small task for change agents, and it is for that purpose that this helpful resource was compiled.

Educators once believed that if we learned what successful facilitators do and then do it, our schools would respond. We developed principles, guidelines, and profiles for leaders to learn and follow; however, we have found that behavioral, linear algorithms of leadership do not govern dynamic, living systems. To be effective in the "chaos" and "disequilibrium" of the 21st century school, we need a new vision of leadership and learning that develops healthy and responsive learning organizations, a vision grounded in both scientific and spiritual disciplines. We need change facilitators who can think, act, and lead with integrative, systemic, and "spirit-full" strategies. The activities presented in this book contribute to such a logic and sequence of change, while also recognizing the intellectual intrigue, the emotional satisfaction, and the social engagement of change.

The role of facilitator is not assumed by one or a few persons in positions at the "top" of the administrative hierarchy. Rather, all members of the organization assume the role of change agents; all participants can become facilitators of change and participate in the continuing process of self- and organizational improvement. This book assists all members of the organization in becoming initiators of change.

Several authors referenced in this book identify trust as the essential condition for change. Without trust, no learning takes place, no change occurs. Without trust, energy is drained from the group in nonproductive ways and may even result in the groups or individuals resorting to creative subversion, subverting the change process to their own mischievous ends. Bruce Williams implies that assuming the identity of a facilitator means developing trust in at least four arenas:

1. Trust in oneself as a facilitator. Only when facilitators trust themselves can they build trust with others. Facilitators consciously plumb their own motives and intentions to assure that they are honorable and altruistic; they place faith in their own abilities to enhance the group's growth; and they trust their capacities to learn from the experience—to monitor, evaluate, and modify themselves as needed. In this book, the motive of change is clearly focused and defined: to enhance student achievement and learning. The facilitator keeps this value clearly in mind as the guiding principle and driving force of the change process—as decisions are made; as

resources of time, money, and energy are allocated; and as progress is assessed. Facilitators set aside personal motives so that they continually focus on the central purpose behind the change: What is best for learners?

2. Trust in relationships with others. The process of change is enhanced when all parties trust and respect each other. This requires that facilitators become expert, nonjudgmental listeners who practice skills such as

- using silence or wait-time to allow group members opportunities to contemplate, process, reflect, and interact;

- asking goal-directed questions that stimulate the group's thinking and further the group to set priorities and make decisions;

- summarizing accomplishments, illuminating ideas, and synthesizing various perspectives in nonjudgmental ways;

- empathizing with group members as they express emotions, fears, and anxieties about the change process;

- clarifying tasks, terminology, values, and concepts and encouraging individuals to become precise in their communication so that all members of the group understand each other and their assigned tasks;

- knowing how to generate and use data as a basis for decision-making and action.

Facilitators not only demonstrate and employ these skills themselves, but they also assist the members of the group in learning to practice, perfect, and assess their use of these skills.

Wise facilitators serve as role models. They model trust and assume that group members are trustworthy. They model the belief that people have their own inner resources to achieve excellence. Through the change process, participants form bonds of interconnectedness and interdependence. It is through such experience that differences are resolved, diversity is valued, beliefs are shared, and people learn to appreciate each other's styles, beliefs, and uniqueness. All parties in the process, stretch to accommodate and transform their thinking and perceptions to form a wider bond of trusting relationships.

3. Trust in the processes of change. As facilitators and their colleagues work together in a nonthreatening, reciprocal relationship, their faith in the change process increases. As groups progress, they become more committed and foster a sense of ownership in the change process.

The wise facilitator is quick to illumine accomplishments that result from the processes and strategies employed. Groups are more willing to commit to strategies that produce satisfactory results. Individuals do not become committed to change because change is mandated or is proven by research to be feasible. Rather, they are convinced because their own experience of success, in their own settings, persuades them. Their attitudes toward innovation improve when they produce evidence of the innovation's effectiveness for themselves.

Furthermore, it is *not* necessary for change agents to become committed to *these* processes per se; it is necessary for change agents to be empowered through these processes. The processes are merely vehicles to emancipate and confirm individual and organizational creativity, to enhance intellectual power, to clarify and translate the organization's mission and goals into action, to build greater awareness of individual members' efficacy, to develop a common vocabulary and shared vision, and to develop the resiliency and stamina needed to confront and overcome obstacles as a team.

Over time, with successive accomplishments, individuals and groups place greater faith in the processes of change and in the facilitator's ability to lead the process. Nothing breeds success like success. Caution, suspicion, and hesitation soon give way to commitment, ownership, volunteerism, and celebration of accomplishment.

Group members realize that the employed processes can be transferred and applied elsewhere. They realize that the intent of these processes is not only to modify the organization but also to modify those who lead the change process—to increase individual participants' capacity to grow intellectually, to learn more about learning, and to increase their capacity for self-change.

4. Trust in the environment. The workplace often signals norms and values that are more influential on staff performance than are the skills, knowledge, and training imparted through staff development. Thus, effective facilitators create, monitor, and maintain a stimulating, mediative, and cooperative environment that enhances the intellectual growth of all members in the learning organization.

This environment gives the organization a sense of congruence, coherence, and integrity. The values inherent in the change processes, the outcomes of the change processes, and the processes of change themselves are as one—continual learning and empowering for all, not only for students, but also for all the members of the educational enterprise. People and organizations do not merely endure change—they seek, sponsor, and enjoy change as a continuing process of lifelong learning. That's what schools are for, and that's what this book is about.

ARTHUR L. COSTA, ED.D.
Halaheo, Hawaii
Professor Emeritus, California State University
Codirector, Institute for Intelligence Behavior,
Berkeley, California

Acknowledgments

A book like this can never come out of a vacuum. Through my work with IRI/SkyLight Training and Publishing, I have been privileged to work with schools throughout the United States and Canada. These schools have been stretching to reach for the new while pondering what practices from the past still work. To all of the teachers, principals, and administrators with whom I have worked, I say thank you. This represents a small token of thanks for the inspiration you have given me.

Some people have graciously given me permission to adapt and use their facilitation tools. I feel compelled to mention them and to indicate how they may be contacted. I adapted practical tool 5 in chapter 6 from Marsha Caplan of the M. Caplan Company, Boulder, Colorado (303-444-9637). For practical tool 5 in chapter 1, I have used a tool created by Bruce E. Honig of San Anselmo, California (415-256-9048). The tool appears in his book *Recipes for Creative TeamWork*. I adapted practical tool 4 in chapter 7 from Allan Holender, president of Educational Fundraising, Inc., Richmond, British Columbia, Canada. His highly acclaimed book, *Private Support for Public*

Education is a valuable resource for schools, school boards, educational foundations, and parent groups. He may be reached at 604-263-9159 for more information about his book or about his workshops or seminars.

Two longtime colleagues form the Institute of Cultural Affairs have also given me permission to use their tools. Mirja P. Hanson, a consultant and facilitator in St. Paul, Minnesota (612-291-5616) provided the theoretical basis for practical tool 4 in chapter 1. Finally, I am grateful for the thinking of another consultant and facilitator, Dorcas Rose, Eastern Regional Director of the Institute of Cultural Affairs (518-273-6797) whose tool I adapted for practical tool 4 in chapter 8.

How can I thank those closest to me who have supported and encouraged me during the winding and intricate steps of putting this together? My partner Jack and my son Daniel and his family have been integral parts of this support. I will name Richard, Jim, Steven, and John to represent the many friends and colleagues who help me appreciate life's journey.

Introduction

As school restructuring efforts are initiated across the country, many schools are calling upon facilitators to guide the change process. Schools and districts often find that the tasks involved in such momentous change are greater than their ability to manage them. In *The New Meaning of Educational Change,* Michael Fullan observes:

> As the kinds of changes introduced to schools have increased in complexity over the last decade—from curriculum- and classroom-based innovations to "restructuring" whole systems—the skills required of schools to implement them have also become more complex. The goals of change are becoming more comprehensive and require greater assistance to achieve. More frequently, schools are turning to internal and external "helpers" to fill gaps in expertise and to assist in charting and implementing courses of action. (1991, p. 215)

Systemic change entails moving from one paradigm to another, from one approach to tasks to another, from one form of organization to another. This shift is complex and unsettling, the course often uncharted. Schools accustomed to a slower change timeline may be adept at handling incremental changes but are thrown into turmoil when faced with demands for drastic restructuring. Consequently, many schools and school districts have hired outside facilitators or have designated internal facilitators to help oversee the change process.

Who plays the roles of the facilitator for change? Many people both inside and outside the school system can play these roles. School administrators, teachers, principals, and community leaders can, as called for, assume any of the many roles of the facilitator.

Most educators are not prepared for facilitating school change. Some educators are designated as facilitators and survive by a "catch-as-catch-can" method. Unfortunately, this method often results in failure and illuminates the fact that facilitators need numerous specific skills to implement successful, lasting, and beneficial changes. This book is dedicated to those assisting in the process of school change and offers a number of helpful tools and approaches.

Many recent reform efforts have been initiated from the state and district levels. These efforts have failed to account for local school needs and limitations. Top-down proposals often create anger, frustration, and resentment (Fullan 1991). For reforms to have enduring value, local constituents, who will implement the changes, need to understand both the need for change and the process of change. They participate in the conception, planning, and implementation of change. This requires that they have the facilitation skills needed for orchestrating and supporting the process, along with an awareness of the resources needed to make the change take hold.

A common misconception among administrators is that local stakeholders have little skill or motivation to implement local school reform. Therefore, administrators often feel they need to hire outside specialists to wring out changes from the local system. "A contrasting view of the process of reform, which is supported by empirical research on change in public and private organizations, emphasizes the role of change agents as facilitators, providers of resources, and consultants" (Astuto et al. 1994, p. 93). In other words, having facilitators work from the bottom up is just as important as having educational reform imposed from the top down. When people at the local level are trained to assume the many roles of facilitator, they can create a "home-grown" capacity for renewal (Astuto et al. 1994). The roles of the facilitator are absolutely essential to successful school change efforts, regardless of whether they are assumed by local people or by outside consultants.

Functions of Facilitators

The vast dimensions of school change require four major functions in facilitators:

- Process Leadership
- Skill Training
- Resource Consulting
- Group Energizing

These four functions are both diverse enough and specific enough that no one person is able to assume them all. The functions may be assumed by a group of three or four or they may be distributed among a group of ten or twelve. Regardless, all four are critical to the implementation of an effective change process.

First, the change process needs a guide, or leader, to keep everyone focused and targeted in their specific duties—the Process Leader. Second, school change requires an instructor, or trainer, to impart new skills demanded by the change process and to enable participants to practice these skills—the Skills Trainer. Third, school change calls for someone to discover how the school can connect with the available resources that support and empower the change process—the Resource Consultant. Last, school change requires tireless work from someone who, week after week, month after month, year after after, finds ingenious ways to summon up the commitment and energy needed for the change process—the Group Energizer. *(Note: For a detailed discussion on each function, see each section introduction—page 2 for process leader, page 46 for skills trainer, page 92 for resource consultant, and page 134 for group energizer.)*

Three Elements of the Change Process

There is broad agreement among writers and thinkers in the area of school change that supports three major elements as aspects of each of the four facilitator functions. These three elements are

1. focusing long-range goals and short-range tasks on *student learning and achievement;*
2. promoting *shared decision-making* among the members of all concerned constituencies; and
3. keeping communication and interaction centered on *visible achievements.*

Student Learning and Achievement

The first element, focusing long-range goals and short-range tasks on student learning and achievement, may be extremely difficult to accomplish amidst the complexity of school reform. At any moment attention can dramatically shift from student learning to staff development or to school safety. However,

> The centrality of student learning is the driving purpose of all activities. . . . Major school improvement efforts can be sustained only when the context promises student learning. Otherwise, the changes in organizational behavior and the struggle

for implementation are likely to be perceived as too stressful to be worthwhile. Essentially, the mission is lost unless learning remains at the core. (Joyce et al. 1993, pp. 19, 20)

No matter what else a school may want to accomplish, student learning is the central goal of systemic change. Change programs that do not focus on student learning are ineffective (David 1991). In other words, creating a system that is committed to student learning is what the change process is all about.

Whatever it takes in the classroom—interactive strategies, cooperative learning techniques, multiple intelligences, problem-based learning methods, critical thinking skills, an integrated curriculum, authentic assessments—teachers need to use tools to transform student learning. Whatever systemic support is needed for these classrooms—site-based decision-making, shared decision-making teams, community and business involvement—community members need to find strategies to transform the system. The facilitator reminds all stakeholders that genuine and tangible improvement in student learning and achievement is the bottom line of all school change efforts.

Shared Decision-Making

The second element in facilitating school change is sharing decision-making power among all stakeholders of the school change process. Many schools, districts, and states attempt to restructure their schools by mandating every step. This imposition of direction from above tends to freeze lower-level participants out of the process. As a principal stated,

> Upon reflection, I realize my leadership style did not allow open participation. Neither was it inclusive nor mutually supportive enough for teachers to buy into the school as co-owners. (Daniels 1990, p. 20)

Top-down, authoritarian decision-making and managing styles can intentionally or inadvertently lessen the participation and creativity needed from other interested parties in the overwhelming process of school change.

What are called for are ways to tap the wisdom and creativity of the entire staff. The issues are too huge and complex to permit responses and solutions to come from a handful when there are huge mental resources and energy to tap in the entire staff. (Williams 1993, p. 61)

Apart from the sheer complexity of implementing school change is the fact that, even though many teachers are engaged in common tasks, their individual jobs are usually lonely and isolated (Sergiovanni 1992). Such isolation results in both duplication of effort and in failure to promote collegiality and shared decision-making. District administrators have discovered that once they move toward shared decision-making, building administrators become willing to experiment with shared decision-making in their own schools.

> One of my joys is to see that pivotal role of principal take on new meaning, new power, and new potential. As I have learned to collaborate with principals and try a new structure to respond to the needs of that group, I see principals willing to emulate that example in their own buildings. (Ingwerson 1990, p. 10)

As shared decision-making between district administrators and building principals, between principals and teachers, and between teachers and parents becomes a reality, the overwhelming tasks surrounding school change become manageable. Teams composed of members from every group of stakeholders then have the chance to offer their input and affect the outcome. Teams that are given the opportunity to recommend *and* the power to create and implement have a chance for success. The facilitator of school change supports this shared decision-making at every level.

Visible Achievements

The third element in facilitating school change is keeping all communication and interaction centered on visible achievements. It is no secret that complaints about the classroom or cristicisms of the latest edicts in school policy abound in teachers' lounges across the country. Many faculty meetings are devoted to discussing the latest state mandates. Many administrator-teacher meetings focus on problem students. Written communication, when it occurs, is often sporadic, incomplete, and inaccurate.

Almost every group of educators at some point brings up the issue of communication, whether written or oral. Fullan argues, "Because change is a highly personal experience, and because school districts consist of numerous individuals and groups undergoing different (to them) experiences, no simple communication is going to reassure or clarify the meaning of change for people" (1991, pp. 198–99).

Effective school change initiatives require accurate, clear, concise, and timely communication. When the pace of change quickens, change implementers find a greater need than ever to know just what is going on.

> In new theories of evolution and order, information is a dynamic element, taking center stage. It is information that gives order, that prompts growth, that defines what is alive. It is both the underlying structure and the dynamic process that ensure life. (Wheatley 1992, p. 102)

Without information, school change participants are left in a vacuum, unsure of how the process is proceeding. Accurate, timely information supports the change process and helps to modify it so that it can continue to succeed.

Successful communication focuses on visible achievements—those events and processes that directly and concretely express the positive changes in the local educational system. When communicated clearly, participants can see exactly what change took place, how it was implemented, and why it worked. Recognizing and announcing achievements generates motivation to produce more victories. Hearing about real successes and accomplishments motivates school change participants to keep going.

Communication that focuses on success can break through the doubt and cynicism that mark many teachers' experiences. Teachers and administrators burn out not only because of long hours but also because they often experience continuous, dismal failure. Dramatic successes encourage more and more energy for the task. Focusing on

visible achievements fosters trust, promotes shared decision-making, increases motivation and commitment, and overcomes the misgivings.

Effective communication allows others objectively to assess progress toward school change. Many times, people are convinced they have incorporated a new practice when very little has been changed or implemented in the classroom. Sharing concrete, visible achievements allows outsiders to determine clearly whether the problem was actually solved or whether the proposed solution fell short of its mark.

Facilitators encourage change teams to produce and share visible achievements. Facilitators help groups create small, tangible achievements to build the momentum for tackling more complex problems.

How to Use This Book

This book proposes twelve fundamental roles for school change facilitators (see Figure 1). These twelve roles emerge from combining the three elements with the four functions. For example, the process leader (function) can take on the role of architect (student learning and achievement element), carpenter (shared decision-making element), or contractor (visible achievements element). Each chapter of this book covers one role with the following format:

- **Role Description**
- **When This Role Is Needed**
- **Skills** that the role requires
- **Practical Tools** with instructions for using them
- **Case Study** describing an instance of how the role was implemented

Each chapter is designed to be read on its own. The reader may read the entire book from cover to cover or may find a chapter that meets the need of the moment. Each chapter provides its own perspective and practical tools. As a further help, the matrix on the following page can guide the reader to the chapter that is most useful at a particular moment.

The Multidimensional Role of the Facilitator in School Change

Functions / Elements	Process Leader	Skills Trainer	Resource Consultant	Group Energizer
Student Learning and Achievement	The **Architect** sees the big picture. • focusing on student learning • expanding traditional boundaries • considering all viewpoints • seeking order instead of control	The **Coach** devises strategies. • choosing relevant curriculum • creating collaborative classrooms • expanding instructional skills and strategies • building a supportive school environment	The **Producer** organizes the project. • battling the scarcity mindset • empowering resource-gathering teams • creating situations that attract resources	The **Conductor** stays true to the score. • aprising the real situation • thwarting attempts to retreat • focusing on the core task
Shared Decision-Making	The **Carpenter** builds consensus. • building trust • focusing on substantial issues • shifting to participatory decision-making • getting input from all stakeholders	The **Quarterback** leads the team. • building communities of learners • creating stakeholder teams • teaching team-building skills	The **Director** overcomes obstacles. • facing obstacles head-on • addressing the true obstacle • enabling teams to challenge obstacles • reflecting on the process	The **Concertmaster** harmonizes the environment. • promoting flexible structures • sharing decision-making power • promoting teamwork • fostering intrinsic motivation
Visible Achievements	The **Contractor** steers the process. • translating vision into action • moving from simple victories to long-term successes • aligning victories with targeted aims	The **Sportscaster** announces the game. • sharing knowledge • reflecting on the process • communicating victories • promoting ownership	The **Promoter** advertises successes. • eliminating isolation and building alliances • connecting schools with outside sources • modeling collaboration • sustaining lifelines of communication	The **Critic** celebrates the performance. • gathering data • spotlighting accomplishments • creating stories

Figure 1

IRI/SkyLight Training and Publishing, Inc.

Part 1

Process Leader

Introduction

Today's organizations have begun to shed the mechanistic, Newtonian worldview that was prevalent in past years (Wheatley 1992). The mechanistic view dictated that objectives and goals be met through sterile, automatic, lock-step tasks.

Growing, thriving companies have adopted a quantum worldview.

> To live in a quantum world, to weave here and there with ease and grace, we will need to change what we do. We will need to stop describing tasks and instead facilitate process. (Wheatley 1992, p. 38)

Modern organizations recognize that they are composed of complex, dynamic processes. They understand that "the process of organizing is much broader and more basic than the task of achieving goals" (Morgan 1986, p. 72).

The process leader is a key player in any organization that desires real change. She moves organizations from mechanistic thinking to process thinking. She orchestrates and conducts processes rather than imposes goals and objectives. She challenges the mechanistic tendency to value stability and pushes for radical reform in approaching tasks and relating to people. She can discern when chaos or upheaval is helpful. School systems that have spent years expanding bureaucratic control and stability need a process leader to guide them through chaos to a more vibrant and responsive organization.

Process leaders "need both technical and change process expertise," because the change process is complex (Fullan 1991, p. 226). They need not be experienced in curriculum, school management, or child development, but they need to know a variety of tools to lead schools from where they are to where they want to be. Currently, schools are inundated with top-down legislative and administrative mandates. Teachers attend numerous inservices on new instructional approaches. Every newly-discerned gap in society is turned over to the schools to solve.

The process leader helps local schools design workable solutions for their unique situations. She brings together administrators, teachers, parents, students, and community members to decide on plans and solutions. She encourages participation and consensus so that she might receive support and commitment for the change process. She attempts to involve all stakeholders in planning and implementing reform.

The process leader may assume three roles: architect, carpenter, or contractor. The architect sees the big picture and focuses on the goal of improving student learning and achievement. The carpenter builds consensus and promotes shared decision-making. The contractor steers the process and puts the focus on creating visible achievements so that those who participate in the process reap the benefits of change.

Chapter 1

The Architect Sees the Big Picture

The Architect is the Process Leader who focuses on student learning and achievement.

Role Description

The architect keeps school teams focused on the big picture—an overall view of what to change and how to work toward change. She does not impose her own ideas on the group; she allows them to discover the big picture for themselves. She keeps pushing for agreement on the big picture as a way to transcend the differences among those holding limited perspectives. She enables people with conflicting viewpoints to look above, beyond, around, and under their views to see the larger perspectives that connect them.

Focusing on Student Learning

The first task of the architect is to remind educators that their central goal is improving student learning and achievement. Teaching and learning focuses on meeting children's needs rather than catering to the needs of everyone else in society (Astuto et al. 1994). While education may validly serve other social, political, and cultural functions: "Education's first responsibilities are to ensure the entitlement of the young to the best that society has to offer and to serve as an agent of

societal improvement and transformation" (Astuto et al. 1994, p. 88).

The educator's essential challenge is to provide each child with a successful learning experience in school. Any other focus diverts attention and energies away from the essential task. The architect of school change keeps groups focused on their crucial task.

Expanding Traditional Boundaries

Most educational institutions are purely preservational (Astuto et al. 1994). In many ways, education is conducted today just as it was one hundred years ago. Society has progressed but schools have not.

School reforms are failing, because educators fail to break out of their preservational, outdated modes of thinking. "Breaking out of our circular loop of reform strategies will require a novel look at the situation" (Deal 1990, p. 7). "The basic causes of the failure [of reform strategies], we will argue, are the narrow limits of imagination that have governed the reform proposals" (Astuto et al. 1994, p. 1).

The architect moves educators out of their traditional, outdated, narrow perspectives. "As Einstein is often quoted as saying: No problem can be solved from the same consciousness that created it. We must learn to see the world anew"

(Wheatley 1992, p. 5). The architect starts by leading teams to perceive the world as it actually is, not as it was in the past, so that teams may devise educational methods that help students participate in the world. If educators do not understand their society, they will find it impossible to envision and to create an education system that helps students participate in society.

Educators who truly wish to transform schools expand their imaginations and ideas about the role education can play in society. They examine new ideas and possibilities for school change and define their purposes and methods to carry out those purposes. They challenge many of the long-held and dear concepts of school that are espoused by parents, local politicians, community members, administrators, teachers, staff, and students (Deal 1990).

The architect helps school change teams think "outside of the bounds." She raises questions that spur teams to do research, to amass data, and to broaden conceptual horizons so that they may discover an overall perspective. She pushes teams to gain the widest perspective possible on their situation (Wheatley 1992). She challenges teams to question their preconceptions about education and educational institutions (Miles and Louis 1990).

Considering All Viewpoints

No one person or group has the final and definitive answers on what education should look like or how it needs to change. Therefore, it is important for the architect to consider the perspectives of all stakeholders in the process of change (Deal 1990). Diversity guarantees success as schools embark on the transformation process. The architect skillfully melds together the diverse viewpoints into a cohesive and powerful whole.

Each school team figures out what is going to work in their local situation.

> First, I no longer believe that organizations can be changed by imposing a model developed elsewhere. So little transfers to, or even inspires, those trying to work at change in their own organizations. Second, and much more important, the new

physics cogently explains that there is no objective reality out there waiting to reveal its secrets. There are no recipes or formulae, no checklists or advice that describe 'reality.' There is only what we create through our engagement with others and with events. Nothing really transfers; everything is always new and different and unique to each of us. (Wheatley 1992, p. 7)

All the stakeholders in a particular situation create school change plans bit by bit, step by step. The architect facilitates this process by teaching teams how to access information from expert sources. She encourages teams to use this information to spark imaginative and creative ideas that fit their own situations. The architect also urges teams to assess their efforts and to integrate new information as it becomes available.

Seeking Order Instead of Control

The change process can be very choatic, but the architect trusts the process even when things seem out of control. The architect enables teams to search for order rather than control in the chaos of the change process.

Teams, in their natural desire for neatness and orderliness, may be tempted to control the change process instead of waiting for a new order to emerge. Instead of allowing the process to move forward, the team may retreat back to the old order, stifling creativeness and responsiveness to the new. The architect urges teams to give up control and search for order within the chaos.

> "What if we could reframe the search? What if we stopped looking for control and began, in earnest, the search for order? Order we will find in many places we never thought to look before. . ." (Wheatley 1992, p. 23)

Teams may also be discomforted by the collapse and disappearance of old structures. As change begins, disintegration of old systems is a necessary step toward the reemergence of a more appropriate form (Wheatley 1992). The architect enables teams to ride the storm and to discern the new forms that are emerging in what seems like either total disintegration or wild, unproductive chaos.

When this Role Is Needed

The architect is needed at the begining of any effort for school change. By raising appropriate questions and by making sure the staff has access to leading articles, books, and videos, the facilitator encourages the school community to look comprehensively at school change. The architect also steps in when teams get detoured—when they spend huge amounts of time and energy on tasks that have little to do with student learning and achievement. The architect encourages the team continually to review their original plans, so that all team members remain focused on their original goals. She ensures that momentary setbacks do not deflect teams from their original path.

Skills

The architect keeps the group focused on the big picture, assuring that student learning and achievement remain the highest priorities. She uses tools such as questions and graphics to illustrate the big picture. She uses strategies that enable the group to expand its thinking and tap into its imagination. The architect is a skilled questioner. Her questions can help a group make leaps in its thinking or discover order amidst chaos.

Practical Tools

The architect enables teams to focus on the big picture by using the following tools:

1. Needs Assessment Grid
2. Resource Analysis
3. Journey Wall
4. Trends Analyis
5. Wishful Thinking Organizer

Practical Tool 1
Needs Assessment Grid

Description

The Needs Assessment Grid helps a group collect and organize information about district and community needs. When all data is gathered, the facilitator leads the group to analyze the information and to make plans for the future.

Example

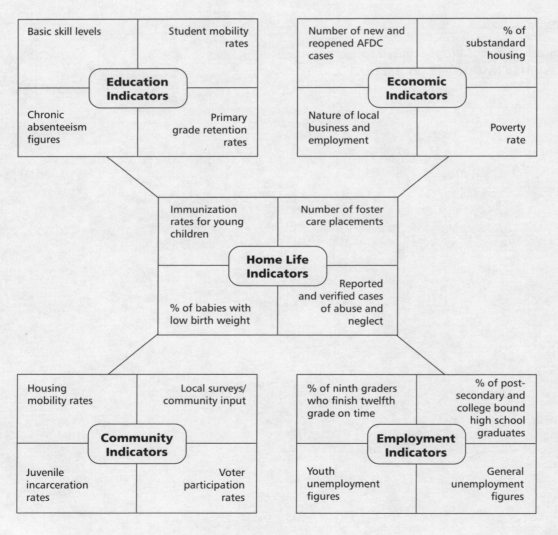

Basic skill levels	Student mobility rates	Number of new and reopened AFDC cases	% of substandard housing
Education Indicators		**Economic Indicators**	
Chronic absenteeism figures	Primary grade retention rates	Nature of local business and employment	Poverty rate

Immunization rates for young children	Number of foster care placements
Home Life Indicators	
% of babies with low birth weight	Reported and verified cases of abuse and neglect

Housing mobility rates	Local surveys/ community input	% of ninth graders who finish twelfth grade on time	% of post-secondary and college bound high school graduates
Community Indicators		**Employment Indicators**	
Juvenile incarceration rates	Voter participation rates	Youth unemployment figures	General unemployment figures

Instructions

Note: A blackline master of the Needs Assessment Grid is provided in Appendix A, page 176.

1. Divide the group into five teams. Assign each team to collect data for one of the five indicators: education, economic, home life, community, or employment.

2. Reconvene the group after teams have had time to collect data.

3. Compile data on a single chart. Display the chart at the front of the room or make copies for each person.

4. Lead a follow-up discussion with these questions:

    a. What data do you remember from what you have read?

    b. Which data are most significant for you?

    c. Which information supported what you knew or sensed before the data collection began?

    d. Which information surprised you?

    e. What messages do the data communicate?

    f. How does the data impact our planning and our future work?

5. Ask an individual or a team to record the answers to these questions and to write a needs assessment report.

Possible Uses

This tool can be used to gather information before any district- or schoolwide strategic planning sessions. Groups may modify the categories of the grid to fit the concerns of their local situation. This tool can enable a group to discover relationships within data clusters and between categories.

Practical Tool 2
Resource Analysis

Description

A group can use this tool to gather and to organize information from written, audio, or video material. The Resource Analysis Chart helps the group connect what they have read, heard, or watched with what they are experiencing or attempting to change in the local school or district.

Examples

RESOURCE ANALYSIS CHART	
Title: "Competencies for Diversity Facilitators"	
Author's Key Ideas	Competency Area 1: Self Knowledge One's personal knowledge, beliefs, and values affect other people. Competency Area 2: Leadership The facilitator promotes diversity. Competency Area 3: Subject-Matter Expertise The facilitator is clear about the goals and implications of diversity. Competency Area 4: Facilitation Skills Skills include preparing, delivering, questioning, listening, maintaining controlling, and managing conflict.
Crucial Insights	The link for all the above four is facilitator style—the ability to genuinely orchestrate procedures, skills, and knowledge.
Local Implications	We need to broaden our subject matter expertise on diversity. We also need to encourage several lead teachers to attend training sessions to expand their facilitation skills.

RESOURCE ANALYSIS GRAPHIC
"Competencies for Diversity Facilitators"

Instructions

Note: A blackline master of the Resource Analysis Chart is provided in Appendix A, page 177.

1. Divide the resources (e.g., articles, books, videotapes, audiotapes) among teams.

2. Display the Resource Analysis Chart, noting the categories—Author's Key Ideas, Crucial Insights, and Local Implications. Ask teams to create a Resource Analysis Chart and a Resource Analysis Graphic that illustrates the major points from the resource.

3. Give the teams time to read, watch, or listen to the material and to complete their reports. (You may choose to assign teams to work on their reports between meetings.)

4. Gather the whole group. Ask each team to post its Resource Analysis Chart and Graphic and to explain what they have learned.

5. Lead a follow-up conversation using these questions:

   a. What ideas or information do you recall from these reports?

   b. Which points seemed most significant to you?

   c. Which information supported what you knew or sensed before hearing the reports?

   d. Which information surprised you?

   e. What is the significance of this information for the work ahead?

6. Ask an individual or a team to record the answers to these questions and write a summary report.

Potential Uses

This tool is particularly useful when you want all group members to begin their thinking from similar starting points. It can also be used to bring the whole group up to date on many sources of information or on a particular area. This tool may be modified so that a group might use it to analyze an oral presentation.

Practical Tool 3
Journey Wall

Description

This tool helps teams see the big picture. It graphically portrays world events, education events, and local school events so that all may be considered in a larger perspective. It enables the group to see connections and implications heretofore unrecognized. By getting an idea of the journey up to now, the group is better equipped to project where the school needs to go next. (This tool is adapted from *More than 50 Ways to Build Team Consensus* by R. Bruce Williams [1993, pp. 44–46].)

Example

THE GREAT JOURNEY OF SERVING THE COMMUNITY						
	A Fresh Start			A Changing Community	A Transformation Challenge	
	1950s	1960s	1970s	1980s	1990s	2000s
World Events	Korean War Cold War Sputnik	Vietnam War JFK Assassinated MLK March on Washington Great Society MLK Assassinated Woodstock	Kent State Oil Embargo Sadat, Begin, Carter	Reagan, Thatcher, Gorbachev Personal Computers AIDS Berlin Wall Down	German Reunification Collapse of USSR Somalia Bosnia Mandela President of S. Africa Rabin, Arafat, Clinton	Examine breakthroughs in former USSR Environmental treaties expanded
Events in Education	Supreme Court Integration	Math/Science Push Johnsons' Cooperative Learning Goodlad's Nongraded Schools	Madeleine Hunter	Glasser's Control Theory	Charter Schools New Ways to Fund Education	Technology enters every classroom Schools as the center of education for whole community
Local School Events	School Built	Open Classrooms	Addition Put On	Basic Skills Emphasis Influx of Asians & Latinos	Cooperative Learning Introduced Multicultural Week Multiage Classroom	High school dropout rate below 1% All students seek education beyond high school

Instructions

1. Determine how far into the past and how far into the future you want to examine. (For example, you might decide to start with the decade of the 50s and go through the decade of the 2010s.)

2. Across the top of a blank wall, list the decades or five-year intervals you are covering. Down the left side of the wall, list three categories: World Events, Events in Education, and Local School Events.

3. Have individuals (if the group is small) or small teams (if the group is large) brainstorm events in all three categories.

4. Ask individuals or teams to write five or six of the most significant events for each category onto 5" x 8" cards, one event per card.

5. Tape the cards on the wall using tape loops. Align the cards in the correct rows and in the appropriate decade or half-decade columns.

6. Allow participants to read the cards and survey the large amount of material.

7. Use the following questions to help the group absorb the mass of information on the wall, connect ideas, and draw conclusions.

    a. Which cards in the World Events row stand out? What relationships or connections do you see among these cards?

    b. Which cards in the Events in Education row grab your attention? What relationships or connections do you see among these cards?

    c. Which cards in the Local School row do you notice? What relationships or connections do you see among these cards?

    d. Where do you see relationships and connections among all three rows?

    e. How does this journey break down into three or four sections? How would you title each of these three or four sections of the journey?

    f. How would you title the whole journey?

    g. How do the discoveries from this activity impact your planning and thinking?

    h. How did this activity alter your perspectives of our school?

Potential Uses

This tool can affirm the perspective of those who have been in the school for a long time and bring new people on board. This activity also enables the group to see the connection between local events and events that transpire in the world around them.

Practical Tool 4
Trends Analysis

Description

This tool lets group members examine a number of trends affecting their institution to determine how they overlap and if they are new, emerging, established, or disappearing. This tool is particularly useful in gauging the timing of the full impact of a trend (e.g., its full impact may be past or its full impact has not been felt yet). (This tool is adapted from Mirja P. Hanson, Consulting and Facilitation, St. Paul, Minnesota.)

Example

Trends in Middle School Education

Boundary — Emerging — Established — Disappearing

Boundary Trends	Emerging Trends	Established Trends	Disappearing Trends
• mainstreamed classes including special-needs students • totally heterogeneous classes • students stay with same teacher teams all through middle school • after school programs for community • whole school/whole year thematic units	• global awareness • staff development • block scheduling • career development plans for individual students • technology (computers)* • teachers teaching more than one subject • interdisciplinary approach to instruction • "politically correct" approach to instruction • more emphasis on assessment and accountablility • increasing questioning of practices and policies by parents (rescues)	• team teaching • summers off • middle school is a transitional period • exact time blocks for all curricular areas • teachers teaching single discipline • having no competition between schools • standardized testing • offering high school credit for certain classes • tracking* • exploratory projects	• middle school being a mini–high school • bell schedules • funding (choices for programs) • lecture for whole class period • retention • feeling kids are brain dead • emphasis on Carnegie units

* indicate key trends

Instructions

1. Divide the group into teams of four or five people.

2. Draw a large trends wave on the wall in the front of the room. (The wave must be wide enough to accommodate four columns of 5"x 8" cards.) Write the four category headings—Boundary Trends, Emerging Trends, Established Trends, and Disappearing Trends—beneath the wave graphic.

3. Explain the four trends using the chart below.

Boundary Trends	Emerging Trends	Established Trends	Disappearing Trends
New horizons	Ideas whose time has come	Status quo	Ideas whose time has gone
"Bleeding edge"	Experimental ideas	"Tried and true"	No longer relevant
Radical ideas	Getting some resource support and backing	Ideas in "good currency"	Outdated way
Emerging ideas	Gaining momentum	Well-funded practices	What's out
	Practices gaining in popularity	Hard to dislodge	
		Standard operating procedures	

4. Prepare 5" x 8" cards of four different colors for each of the four sections. Distribute the first batch of cards (several cards per team) and have each team brainstorm some Disappearing Trends, writing their choices on the cards. Repeat this step for the Established Trends, Emerging Trends, and Boundary Trends.

5. Ask each team to place their cards under the appropriate columns on the wall. After all cards are posted, allow the group to study the cards.

6. Lead a follow-up conversation using these questions:

   a. What significant trends do you notice?

   b. Which trends had you forgotten until you saw them on the wall display?

   c. Which trends were you surprised to see in the display?

   d. What do you notice as you examine the whole wall? What does this whole picture of the trends communicate?

   e. Have you participated in any of these trends?

   f. Where do you see connections within a column or between different columns?

   g. What trends merit encouragement and support?

    h. What opportunities does this display of trends present to us? What threats does this display suggest?

    i. What are some implications for planning and thinking?

    j. How has your thinking been altered by participating in this activity? How has the thinking of our group been changed by engaging in this activity?

7. Assign an individual or a team to record the answers to the questions and write a summary report.

Potential Uses

This activity can address the concerns of two distinct groups—those who are ready to move with the latest innovation and those who are reluctant to jump onto the latest bandwagon. It can also enlighten those who have failed to "see the handwriting on the wall," enabling them to make some necessary leaps in thought, imagination, and commitment.

IRI/SkyLight Training and Publishing, Inc.

Practical Tool 5
Wishful Thinking Organizer

Description

The Wishful Thinking Organizer enables groups to devise fresh approaches and to re-examine tradition-bound approaches. This tool uses a variety of media to jar the minds of group members so that they can grasp imaginative and creative solutions. (This tool is adapted from the Combining Teams tool in *Recipes for Creative TeamWork* by Bruce E. Honig [1991].)

Example

Focus or Issue: How can our teachers have more professional developing, training, and planning time?

Logical Thinkers List	Creative Thinkers List
1. Pay teachers for an additional 3–4 weeks after school ends or before it begins	1. Hold informative but engaging assemblies to free half the teachers
2. Get grants to pay for substitutes	2. Tap community and business resources
3. Bank time and send students home early every other week	3. Initiate year-round school
4. Experiment with block scheduling	

Creative Workable Connections

1. Don't send students home; have hands-on experiments and experiences led by community and businesses with some teacher guidance

2. Direct Administrative support in the classroom to free up teachers

3. Under teacher supervision, use older students to work with younger students

4. Student community service projects/learning

Instructions

1. State the general focus or the specific issue that the group is to target.

2. Form two teams: a logical-thinking team and a creative-thinking team. Assign a meeting area for each team. In each meeting area, provide appropriate art and music. For the logical team, you may choose realistic art and classical music, and for the creative team, you may choose impressionistic or modern art and new age or space music.

3. Restate the focus or issue. Allow time for individual brainstorming.

    a. Individuals in the logical team can brainstorm using one of the following stems:

    What needs to happen here is . . .

    The research indicates that we need to . . .

    Given what has been going on in the school, the next step is . . .

    b. Individuals in the creative team can brainstorm using one of the following stems:

    I wish . . .

    What I really want is . . .

    Wouldn't it be great if . . .

    Looking at this piece of art (or listening to this music), it occurs to me that . . .

4. Ask individuals to share their thinking with their team and direct teams to create a list of responses.

5. Post responses and request that teams explain their responses.

6. Divide the group into new teams of three or four. (Be sure teams include a mixture of logical team members and creative team members.) Ask teams to synthesize ideas from the Logical Thinkers List with the ideas from the Creative Thinkers List to create a Workable Possibilities List that includes new, creative, and workable solutions.

7. Ask teams to share their ideas. Choose ideas and solutions that seem most appropriate and begin planning how to implement them.

Potential Uses

This activity is useful when the group gets stuck, when nothing seems possible, and when members suggest that everything has already been tried. This activity can be conducted around a general concern (e.g., preparing students for the next century) or around a particular concern (e.g., relaxing the rigid schedule or getting parents involved with the school).

Case Study

Laying Tracks to the New

A long-standing military academy on the East Coast embarked on a process of restructuring that included rethinking their mission. Much tradition surrounded their decades of service as a military academy.

The architect (facilitator) stepped into this situation and began to share her ideas of what a totally new academy might look like. She brought in speakers and workshop leaders to challenge the staff members' thinking. She also held strategic planning sessions for the staff.

Because the architect had caused the group to see the big picture, the leaders and staff decided to reimage their school as a global learning community. They expanded the grades offered from 9–12 to pre-K–12. They offered high school students the option of participating in the military academy program or the prep school program. They marketed their school to certain Asian countries and many Asian students have since enrolled. Other foreign students whose parents live in the area have also enrolled. Currently, there is a waiting list for many of the grades in this school.

The leaders and staff at this academy accepted a creative mindset when they imagined the school as a global learning community. They chose not to try to breathe new life into the traditional image of a military academy. This school was transformed because the educators were able to step back and see a large enough picture which honored the past and moved the school into an exciting future.

The Carpenter Builds Consensus

The Carpenter is the Process Leader who focuses on shared decision-making.

Role Description

The carpenter builds consensus among administrators and teachers and among all stakeholders in the school change process. The carpenter honors and considers the hopes and dreams of every participant and guides the group to mold its own purposeful vision. He uses tools and processes to create and support shared decision-making. He builds trust among teachers and their leaders and ensures that decision-makers receive all the information they need to make wise judgments. He helps teams make significant choices about crucial issues.

Building Trust

Trusting People

To build consensus, the carpenter trusts the people with whom he is working. He profoundly believes that sound group decisions are better than individual decisions.

> When asked if she had any advice for new principals, Susan replied, 'Deep down in your heart, you have to trust the process of coming to consensus. There are *many* right

answers. Staff members are at many levels of readiness and energy.' (Ellis 1994, p. 59)

Many administrators say that they value consensus and participation, but their speech belies them: "You can't do that because. . . "; "We talked about that last year and it won't work"; "Well, I don't really like that idea"; "You won't be able to do that, because I just got this memo last week saying . . ." These comments tell the group that the administrator does not trust them. If the administrator knows that certain plans or ideas will not work, he states this clearly *before* the ideas are mentioned as possibilities by the group.

Even when administrators trust teachers to make decisions, many teachers resist taking an active decision-making role. Assuming responsibility and accountability for making choices can be frightening and discomforting (Goldman and O'Shea 1990). Teachers who have never been allowed to make decisions find it difficult to trust one another and often defer decisions back to the adminstrator. The carpenter gradually guides teachers into decision-making. As teachers and groups become more skilled in making choices, they begin to trust themselves and others and they willingly accept more responsibility.

Sharing Information

The carpenter also builds trust by sharing information. He ensures that all of the crucial data needed to make a sound decision has been freely offered to the group. He also allows the group adequate time to absorb and process the information.

Many administrators and principals do not realize how much information they have that others do not (Foster 1990). Some administrators realize that they have much information, but they consciously withhold it so that they might sabotage group efforts. They either prevent groups from reaching a sound decision or use the information as a trump card to negate any work a group has done.

The carpenter seeks to transform the administrator or principal from a resource protector into a resource sharer. As leaders share information, they empower teachers to become decision-makers, and they lessen the pressure of decision-making to allow groups to come to collaborative, sound decisions.

Focusing on Substantial Issues

The carpenter guides groups to make decisions about tough issues. While it may take time for groups to get accustomed to making choices, groups want to wrestle with significant concerns that have important ramifications; otherwise, they will feel they are wasting time.

Cynicism quickly develops if groups are prevented or shielded from working through significant concerns.

> It does little good for a district that commits to shared decision making to leave few areas of perceived freedom in which decisions can be made. Progress in this domain is being made one decision at a time. Over time, enough incidents should clarify and expand the range of possibilities for meaningful shared decision making. (Johnston 1990, p. 48)

Most groups become more committed when they know they have been given authentic, real-life, heavy-duty tasks and decisions (Foster, 1990).

Shifting to Participatory Decision-Making

The carpenter encourages schools to shift from top-down to participatory decision-making. When lateral relationships replace top-down, vertical relationships, successful consensus-building organizations are formed. Amidst the push for school change, flexibility and responsiveness have emerged (Morgan 1986). Administrators have adopted a style that supports others in making decisions and have improved their skills in building consensus and in relating to people (Goldman and O'Shea 1990).

The carpenter uses various tools and skills to foster lateral decision-making. He convinces leaders that participatory, collaborative styles unleash energy (Astuto et al. 1994). He teaches them "the elements of participative/collaborative style . . . persuading more than ordering, team building, seeking input from others, showing political sensitivity, and sharing recognition" (Simpson 1990, p. 36). He stresses that objectives and plans can be meaningful to employees only when they have participated in making them (Wheatley 1992).

Getting Input from All Stakeholders

Finally, the carpenter builds consensus by getting input from *all* stakeholders—teachers, parents, students, administrators, community members, business representatives. All who are affected need to be consulted to transform education.

In the past, schools were homogeneous—everyone embraced the same cultural traditions and values. Today, schools are built on diversity and heterogeneity; consequently, the carpenter considers all of the perspectives represented in the community. He looks between, underneath, around, behind, and beyond what all stakeholders are saying and discovers how their viewpoints are connected. The carpenter molds disparate elements into a masterpiece that captures the spirit and focus of all the stakeholders.

When this Role Is Needed

The carpenter steps in when an organization seems fragmented or has an unclear direction or confused focus. He may also assume this role as a school shifts from autocratic, top-down leadership into participatory, collaborative decision-making. The carpenter assists organizations who wish to get all stakeholders' involved in the school change process. He uses his expertise to build consensus out of many contradictory or conflicting perspectives.

Skills

The carpenter assists groups to increase their experience and confidence, as well as tools for consensual decision-making. His fundamental skill is to communicate trust in the group and in the consensus-building process. Through actions and words, he communicates that he willingly backs the group's decisions. He honors each individual's dignity. He acknowledges everyone's contributions and honors disagreements. He believes in the process of consensus building and in the ability of the group to affect real change.

Practical Tools

The carpenter builds consensus among school change advocates by using the following tools:

1. Decision-Making Phase Chart
2. Beliefs and Principles Workshop
3. Snapshots Gallery
4. Cardstorming Chart
5. Parking Lot Strategy

Practical Tool 1
Decision-Making Phase Chart

Description

This tool enables a school or a district to create a chart for expanding decisions to the local team level. The chart plots a course for the gradual transference of responsibility from the administrative level to site-based teams. This tool also clarifies which decisions may never appropriately be transferred. For optimal use, do this activity in groups with representatives from all three levels—administrative, principal, and site-based teams.

Example

YEARS DECISIONS	1996–97	1997–98	1998–99	1999–2000	2000–2001
District Goals	A	A & P	A & P	A & P & S	A & P & S
School Goals	A & P	P & S	P & S	P & S	P & S
Staff Development Emphasis	A	A & P	P & S	P & S	P & S
Site Budget Allocations	A	A	A & P	P & S	P & S
Hiring/Firing Teachers	P	P	P & S	P & S	P & S
Materials Purchasing	A	A	S	S	S
Curriculum	A	A	A	S	S
Publicity	A	A	P & S	P & S	P & S
Hiring/Firing Principals	A	A	A	A	A & S

A = Administrator   P = Principal   S = Site-Based Teams

Instructions

1. Specify how many years this chart is to cover (e.g., three years, four years, five years, six years). On a wall in front of the room, post 5" x 8" cards on chart paper to represent these years.

2. Divide the group into teams of three or four to brainstorm the types of decisions currently made in the district.

3. Ask each team to report its ideas. Write the names of the decisions on 5" x 8" cards. Place the cards on the left side of the wall chart.

4. Request that teams consider several of the decision categories and determine when power will be transferred and who will assume power.

5. Direct teams to write their decisions on the chart, using A for administration, P for principal, or S for site-based team. Each team should explain the rationale for its recommendations.

6. Ask clarifying questions as needed. Solicit questions, comments, suggestions, and changes. Repeat until all the categories and team reports have been covered.

7. Close with some processing questions:
   a. What have we accomplished?
   b. How will this transfer of decision-making power impact the district?
   c. What enabled us to agree on the elements of this chart?

Possible Uses

School panels discussing restructuring or school reform can use this tool to open up the decision-making process for conversation. This tool may convince skeptics that the district or the school is serious about moving from traditional top-down direction to shared decision-making. This activity may be conducted with smaller teams before the large group meets to finalize the chart.

Practical Tool 2
Beliefs and Principles Workshop

Description

This workshop helps teams discover their underlying beliefs and principles so that they may come to consensus on how to work toward change.

Example

Beliefs and Principles about Redesigning Curriculum			
Student-Centered Focus	**Important Components**	**Resource Support**	**Stakeholder Involvement**
All students can learn	Our students need to be familiar with computer technology	Stay within our budget	Parents deserve a say
All students deserve to be challenged	Basic skills are foundational	Look for a variety of resource sources	All stakeholders need to have a voice
	Higher order thinking skills need to be included	Financially doable	

Instructions

1. Pose the question, "What beliefs and principles do we want the process and the product to embody?"

2. Allow participants to reflect on the question for three or four minutes.

3. Divide the group into seven or eight teams of three or four. Ask participants to share their answers in their teams. Have teams choose the most important five or six beliefs and principles and legibly write each one on a 5" x 8" card.

4. Solicit the best cards from each team. Read the cards and put them in random columns on the front wall. Ask the group to let you know when cards are similar so that you can group similar cards in the same column.

5. Direct the teams to turn in another card that is the most different from any card up on the wall so far. Read these cards and display them at random.

6. Ask the group to organize the cards in clusters and to suggest working titles for the clusters.

7. Label each cluster with a number, letter, or symbol.

8. Have teams categorize their remaining cards, putting the appropriate number, letter, or symbol on the front of each card. Assure the teams that they do not need to force any card into a cluster—the whole group can decide where to place cards that the team is having a hard time categorizing.

9. Request that teams turn in their remaining cards. Read them and put them on wall in the appropriate clusters.

10. Ask the group to suggest titles for each cluster. After all the titles have been polished, reread the original question and note the cluster titles that answer the question.

11. Process the activity with these questions:

    a. What beliefs and principles speak to you?

    b. What have we accomplished in this activity?

Possible Uses

This is another strategy to use when you are working with a hot topic and feel that the group is not ready to initiate serious planning. This tool helps unite groups that feel divided and fragmented. It provides a positive experience of connection without focusing on the hot topic directly. Very often, this positive experience moves the group to begin talking about the hot topic.

Practical Tool 3
Snapshots Gallery

Description

This tool is useful when conflict emerges, because it moves communication from the verbal to the visual, from an argument framed in words to a picture or a graphic that poses a solution. *[Note: Using Gardner's insights on multiple intelligences, the presupposition behind this activity is that conflict often emerges in the verbal/linguistic arena and will never be solved in that arena when emotions run high. By bringing in a visual/spatial element of the graphic and restricting the use of words, there is a chance for connection and communication that could not take place in the verbal realm. Interpersonal dimensions are also tapped and foster constructive dialogue. Once this activity has been completed, the group may return to the verbal realm and continue talking and planning.]*

Example

The following categories might arise when dealing with the explosive topic of inclusion.

	Involve All Stakeholders in Solution	Put the Child First
	Create Strong Support for the Classroom Teacher	Establish an Ongoing Monitoring System
	Train all Teachers on Strategies and Approaches to Inclusion	Initiate a Pilot Demonstration Class

Instructions

1. When conflict erupts, stop the discussion and suggest that another approach be used.

2. Divide participants into teams of three or four. Distribute chart paper and magic markers of various colors. Prepare ten border cards (to use in step 6).

3. Ask each team to create a picture, graphic, or image that has elements of a solution to this explosive issue. Explain that they cannot include words in their image.

4. Allow teams twenty minutes to create a picture, graphic, or image. Walk around and coach any group that is having difficulty.

5. Lead the group through this reporting process:

   a. Each team displays its graphic.

   b. Everyone, except the members of the team that created the graphic, describes what they see in the graphic and what solution elements are represented.

   c. The team that created the graphic adds their comments.

6. Put up ten title border cards flanking all the graphics and ask the group, "What are some of the common themes leading to a solution that you noticed in these graphics?" Write these responses on the title border cards.

7. When you finish writing the title cards, ask the following questions:

   a. What have we accomplished?

   b. What happened during this activity?

   c. What happened to us as a group during this activity?

Possible Uses

There are times when a group reaches an impasse—emotions run high and dicussion becomes sharp and hostile. The vested interests of various parties seem locked in unresolvable conflict. The intent of this activity is not to resolve the issue, but to bring groups back to a place where they can resume talking about it.

Practical Tool 4
Cardstorming Chart

Description

While this tool takes practice to use well, it is by far one of the most helpful tools in bringing together ideas from diverse perspectives and creating consensus. The group brainstorms ideas, writes the ideas onto 5" x 8" cards, and then clusters the cards to determine the major concerns. Deciding how to name the clusters also helps create consensus. (This tool is adapted from *More than 50 Ways to Build Team Consensus* by R. Bruce Williams [1993, pp. 25–27].)

Example

Practical Vision						
Confident Student Initiative	**Positive Enthusiastic Attitude**	**Upbeat, Regular Communication**	**Supportive, Quality, Peer Collaboration**	**Shared Community Responsibility in the School**	**Innovative Curriculum Oriented toward Student Needs**	**Exemplary Facilitators with Community Input**
Students tapping resources	Happy, smiling faces; working together	Student work displayed	Shared planning time	Parents and community leaders in classroom	Teach decision-making responsibility	Crews finishing new windows
		Reception area (with student lounge and display board)	Teachers sharing information and classes	Vote yes for tax levy	Teach how to learn	
	Students and teachers enjoying learning	T-charts and team logos	Training of teachers	Business curriculum connection	Electives for average and below average students	New building
Student-run assembly		School-community confidence	Cooperative learning groups	Parents assume responsibility		
			Faculty idea exchange	Family resource center	Positive coping mechanisms	New library
	Energized teacher and students	Use of positive reinforcers	Faculty works together			
			Teacher cooperation	Community school programs	Meet needs of all students	
Students on task		Student social skills	Cooperative education in classroom	Parents as tutors		Separate two schools
	School spirit	"I can" attitude		Parent volunteers	Global-environmental curriculum	
			Planning time			

From: Summers County Schools, West Virginia, November 1991

Instructions

1. Prepare a focus question for the group to brainstorm. Pose the question to the group. Discuss the context with the group briefly, indicating why you find this question particularly relevant.

2. Give participants time to think. (This ensures that both quick and deliberate thinkers have ample time to organize their thoughts.)

3. Create teams of two, three, or four. Ask individuals to share their ideas with their team. (This gives people "air time" in small groups, permitting early feedback to their ideas and relieving the need to use whole-group time to air their ideas.)

4. Guide teams to choose five or six of their best ideas. (All together, you need thirty-five to forty ideas. Divide that number by the number of teams you have to figure out how many ideas to solicit from each team.) Instruct teams to write these ideas onto 5" x 8" cards, one idea per card. Suggest that they use just three to four words per card so that the cards remain legible.

5. Direct teams to turn in one or two of their best ideas. Tape the cards on the wall in random columns.

6. Ask teams to turn in ideas that differ greatly from those already posted.

7. Ask the whole group to name any connections they see between the ideas. Cluster these cards together. Ask groups to temporarily title the emerging clusters. Ask for more ideas until five or six clusters appear.

8. Label the clusters with a number, letter, or symbol.

9. Call for the remaining ideas, asking teams first to write the number, letter, or symbol on the cards if they fit readily into an existing cluster. Explain that they need not force an idea into a category. The whole group can decide what to do with the ideas that don't seem to fit into a category. Shift and move cards as the group gains greater clarity.

10. Urge the group to devise clear, concise, accurate titles for each category.

11. Assign an individual or team to type up and distribute the chart so that the group might reflect upon it and polish it.

Possible Uses

This activity is extremely useful when people are reluctant to contribute ideas for one reason or another. It is also helpful in situations where a few people tend to dominate the group discussion. The graphic nature of this tool keeps people focused on very complex topics. This is an excellent way to pull together ideas when perspectives are very diverse or contradictory.

Practical Tool 5
Parking Lot Strategy

Description

This activity enables a group to see what progress they are making in coming to consensus. It also helps them identify items on which they still have not reached agreement.

Example

Brainstorm Question:
How can our school increase
our instructional prowess this year?

Items that Have Met Consensus

1. Plan more lessons as teams
2. Use collaborative groupings
3. Initiate cross grade groupings
4. Use more lessons that utilize a variety of multiple intelligeces
5. Initiate peer coaching program
6. Expand peer tutoring program
7. Get training in authentic assessment
8. Analyze students weak points from standardized tests
9. Share teaching successes monthly
10. Use inservice days to provide additional training

Parking Lot
• Paint the hallways
• Add 2 more desks to Room 215
• Decide date for Fall Open House
• Turn in grant proposal by September 20

Instructions

1. Request that teams present reports on the work they have been conducting and post their products on the wall. Remind the whole group *not* to comment on reports at this stage.

2. Ask the group which reports meet with consensus and which do not. For visual effect, you might highlight items that have met consensus.

3. Write the consensus items on the left side of a piece of chart paper. Write the names of the items which do not meet with consensus on the right side in a box labeled The Parking Lot.

4. Begin discussing the "parked" items. Start with the two or three that you think are relatively easy to settle.

5. Move on to more difficult items after the group has successfully solved some issues and feels confident.

6. If one or two items remain and appear too difficult, ask what information would be needed for consensus to be reached. Assign teams to come up with possible solutions to present at the next meeting.

Possible Uses

This tool is particularly useful when an item awaiting consensus is very complex and has many components. This strategy can enable progress to be made on most of the items and can precisely target the remaining issues. This helps when a group feels overwhelmed at the complexity of an issue or feels that it is not progressing on any issues.

Case Study

Order from Diverse Ideas

An elementary school had decided to apply for a grant. The grant required that the group 1) conduct a needs assessment, 2) use the results of the assessment to formulate a project focus, and 3) propose three implementation plans.

The group asked a carpenter (facilitator) to help them with this process. The carpenter's first action was to lay out a step-by-step process for the group to follow as it conducted the assessment, formulated a focus, and determined implementation plans. He encouraged the group to begin pulling together data to be used in the needs assessment. He provided the teams with a report form to collect the data.

When teams had amassed a large amount of data, the carpenter directed the teams to produce a large report on butcher paper. At the next meeting, he asked teams to hang their reports on the wall so that the whole group could survey all of the data. He encouraged all participants to note any needs that the data seemed to bring out.

The carpenter then created a visual and asked participants to write in any needs they had recognized. From that the carpenter led them in pulling together an informed profile of their school, consisting of what the situation was (based on the data of the needs assessment) and what possible recommendations would be. With that informational base, the carpenter asked the group to target the top ten needs and to determine a project focus that was congruent with those needs.

The carpenter divided the group into three teams and asked each team to formulate the three implementation emphases. As each of the teams shared their three emphases, the carpenter listed them on a piece of butcher paper at the front of the room. The group then decided which three emphases were most feasible.

After completing the entire process together, the participants said, "At last we have a clear focus now. At last we see how to start making that focus happen." They were satisfied because they all had participated in the decision.

Chapter 3

The Contractor Steers the Process

The Contractor is the Process Leader who focuses on communicating visible achievements.

Role Description

The contractor's job is to help the organization create visible victories. She urges school change teams to craft a workable vision and to move from planning into implementing. She designs the step-by-step process that helps the school enact its reform. She helps teams recognize victories and successes from the implemented changes. She uses tangible victories to motivate and energize teams to take on more complex restructuring tasks. She knows that people need to see visible victories; therefore, she seeks a balance between formulating a solid theoretical foundation and producing visible signs of success.

Translating Vision into Action

The contractor knows when it is time to move from planning into implementing. Enthusiasm wanes when educators see no visible fruits for their research and study. They begin to wonder if they are wasting their time talking and planning and begin to feel that nothing will ever happen.

Some teams may feel uncertain about how to take the first steps toward school transformation

(Miles and Louis 1990); therefore, they may revert to planning instead of moving into action. Other teams may jump into action before they have hammered out a workable vision and a focused plan. The contractor's task is to discern when teams are ready to implement and to encourage teams to move into action even when they feel uncomfortable.

The contractor may move groups from planning to action by using five key questions (developed by the Institute of Cultural Affairs):

1. *Practical Vision.* What will our organization look like five years from now?

2. *Underlying Contradictions.* What stands in the way of the realization of our vision?

3. *Strategic Directions.* What arenas of activity will resolve the contradiction and release the practical vision to come into being?

4. *Systematic Actions.* What specific actions will implement the Strategic Directions?

5. *Implementation Timeline.* What steps are required to implement this action? How will they get done? Where? By whom? By when? (Spencer 1989, pp. 97–98)

These questions naturally move groups from choosing a vision to implementing a concrete, workable plan.

Moving from Simple Victories to Long-term Successes

At the beginning of the implementation stage, the contractor pushes for simple, visible victories. She knows that it is crucial to establish momentum in a school that is just beginning the implementation process.

Following a step-by-step process may be a very new experience for educators. Teachers who have worked solely in their classrooms may find working with others to be risky and frightening. Beginning with simple, achievable projects builds the confidence and skills needed to proceed to more complex projects (Goldman and O'Shea 1990). Completing projects sparks the motivation of the whole school as well as the team carrying it out. Others volunteer to participate in the school change process.

Aligning Victories with Targeted Aims

The contractor continually makes sure that victories remain connected to the original goals and aims. The contractor does not push for victories for victory's sake; they must tie in with the original plans. Achievements are motivating. The danger is that the excitement causes individuals and teams to go off in all directions (Byham 1992).

The contractor enables the teams to keep implementation focused on targeted aims and goals. She continually reminds teams of their stated goals and purposes and urges teams to examine how their implementation plans align with their goals. Genuine change is possible only when teams stay on course; tangents waste energy and time. The contractor coordinates the victories so that they impact the task of school transformation.

The contractor closely monitors the change process as it unfolds. She helps teams navigate around and through uncertainties, interruptions, resistances, and obstacles. She knows that genuine change requires timely action in the present

(Peters 1987) and long-term commitment to the future (Johnston et al. 1990). Therefore, the contractor keeps one eye on the long-range goals for significant, systemwide change and keeps the other eye on short-range innovations and experimentation.

When this Role is Needed

The facilitator adopts this role when an organization seems stuck and is unsure of how to progress. The contractor's emphasis on visible victories enables the group to perform small steps so that they then gain confidence to forge ahead. The contractor helps school change teams that are hesistant to move from planning to implementing. She knows that doubts and questions can be solved by doing the job and by creating visible victories.

Skills

The contractor carries school change teams from planning to implementing. She uses her abilities to listen and perceive to gauge when the group has captured just enough of the vision so that it might move into planning implementation steps. The contractor is also skilled in discerning benchmarks that signify success. Without these marking points, groups do not know when they have made progress.

Practical Tools

The contractor moves teams from planning into implementing by using these tools:

1. Visible Achievement Wheel
2. Video Clips
3. Process Chart
4. Year's Accomplishment Chart

Practical Tool 1
Visible Achievement Wheel

Description

The Visible Achievement Wheel helps the group choose an achievement that sends a positive message to the school community. This tool enables the group to devise an achievement that grabs the community's attention. The tool focuses on creating a schoolwide achievement.

Example

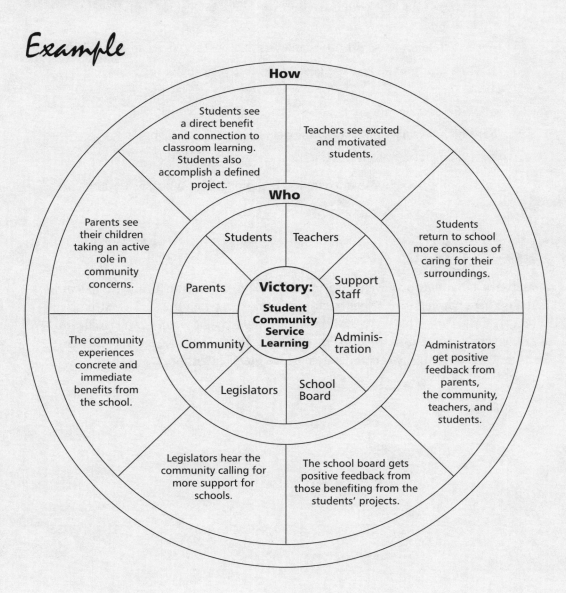

Instructions

Note: A blackline master of the Visible Achievement Wheel is provided in Appendix A, page 178.

1. Remind the group why they are choosing an achievement that sends a positive message to the community.

2. Distribute copies of the Visible Achievement Wheel to all participants.

3. Divide the group into several teams. Ask each team to suggest two or three visible achievements. List all suggestions on butcher paper in front of the room.

4. Direct each team to choose one suggestion and to fill in the wheel. Assign one member per team to create a large wheel on chart paper. Have the team put their data on the large wheel, so they can share their information with the whole group.

5. Invite each team to report on its analysis and post its wheel so all can see it.

6. Lead the group to choose the best achievement by using the following questions:

   a. Which victory affects the most stakeholders?

   b. Which victory significantly impacts students and teachers?

   c. Which victory promotes the most classroom learning?

7. Ask the group to choose one victory. Begin planning the steps for implementing that victory.

Possible Uses

Sometimes a dramatic achievement is needed to signal that something is happening, that a new era has begun. The contractor uses this tool when the staff is extremely discouraged. Organizing this focus and accomplishing a major victory can significantly alter the staff's mood. Also, advertising a visible achievement that impacts the students and the community can generate positive media attention.

Practical Tool 2
Video Clips

Description

The video clips tool is similar to the Snapshots Gallery tool (chapter 2, tool 3). While the Snapshots Gallery tool moves teams out of conflict, the Video Clips tool helps teams move from researching to implementing. Teams that have "overvisioned" themselves find it useful to stop talking and start creating visual pictures of where they want to go. As in the Snapshots Gallery, this tool uses Gardner's insights on multiple intelligences to move participants from the verbal/linguistic mode to the visual/spatial mode.

Example

Child-Centered Relevant Curriculum	Decision-Making Implementation Teams
Diverse Instructional Strategies	Increased Opportunities for Student Responsibility
Parent/ Community Classroom Involvement	Student Involvement in the Community
Community of Learners Atmosphere	Multiple Scores of Resources

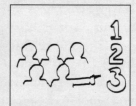

Instructions

1. Divide participants into teams of three or four. Distribute chart paper and magic markers of various colors. Prepare ten border cards (to use in step 5).

2. Have each team create a picture, graphic, image, or video clip that dramatizes some aspect of the discussions they have been having about what they want for their school.

3. Allow teams ten to fifteen minutes to create a picture, graphic, image, or video clip. Walk around and coach any group having difficulty.

4. Have each group choose a reporter. Direct reporters to present their team's graphic to the whole group and to post it on the wall.

5. Put up ten title border cards flanking all the graphics and ask the group, "What are some of the common themes running through these pictures?" Write these responses on the title border cards.

6. When the title border cards are finished, ask the group, "Which one of these titles are you personally drawn to?"

7. After hearing some of the comments, read the title cards and note that these are important pieces of the group's vision.

Possible Uses

This tool is crucial to use when the contractor runs into a group that has "over-visioned" itself with months of research, studies, debates, and workshops. When participants overvision they become cynical and resistant and tired of talking. The discerning contractor can use a Video Clips tool whereby people translate their hopes into a visual, a graphic, or a picture. This is a great tool to use when many of the participants tend to be abstract in their thinking or their discussion. Also, when a situation has been overburdened with working on abstract goals and objectives, this pulls people back into experiencing the concrete implications of their discussions. This is also a great tool to use when there have been some conflicts preventing the planning to proceed.

Practical Tool 3
Process Chart

Description

The Process Chart helps the contractor or the group determine what stage of implementation they are in. The contractor may use the analytical questions herself or pose the workshop questions to the group.

Example

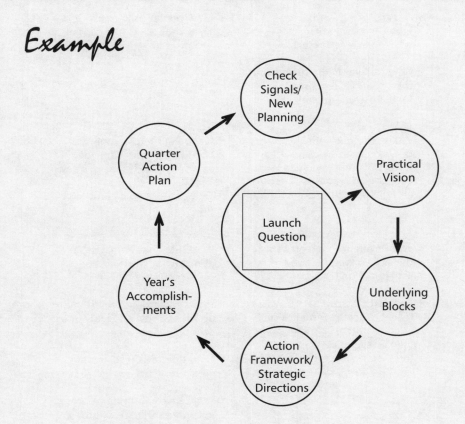

Instructions

1. Consult the chart on page 40. Use the analytical questions to determine where the group is and how much attention they need to devote to each area. Then, use the workshop questions with the group.

   a. Analytical questions: Use these questions on your own to analyze the group's progress. The questions can help you gauge how much time and effort is needed in each step. For example, a group that has spent two years researching and discussing their vision may only need a twenty-minute debriefing to pull together the major elements of the vision. A group that has done little research or discussion may need to engage in a two hour visioning session.

b. Workshop questions: Pose these questions to the group so that they may determine where they are in restructuring process. You may choose to use the questions to do a full cardstorming workshop (chapter 2, tool 4) or to engage in a brainstorming session.

	Analytical Questions	**Workshop Questions**
Needs Analysis	• Has the group gathered enough data to help them see what the real situation is? • How familiar is the group with the situation, community, families, students, etc.?	• (See Needs Assessment Grid from chapter 1, tool 1)
Community Input	• What materials indicate that the group has held input forums or conducted surveys to hear the educational concerns and desires of the community?	• What are the community's hopes and desires for the school system? • What are the most crucial priorities for our schools?
Research Phase	• What evidence indicates that the staff is well-read in the latest educational research? • As I visit classrooms, do I see teachers using strategies such as cooperative learning, multiple intelligences, critical thinking skills, curriculum integration, authentic assessment, etc.?	• What does the research say about what works in the classroom? • What does the research say about the best approaches to school management? • How does this research affect your situation? • What research findings are applicable to this situation?
Practical Vision	• What evidence indicates that the school has forulated a vision statement or a mission statement? • What changes do staff members hope for?	• What changes in the next three years will indicate that we are accomplishing our mission? • What will we hear people saying in three years that would indicate that we have been successful?

(Continued on next page)

	Analytical Questions	**Workshop Questions**
Underlying Blocks	• Does the group seem over-whelmed? • What percentage of the conversation focuses on struggles and blocks? • How resistant are group members to new possibilities?	• What are the obstacles, road-blocks, or hindrances that stand in the way of implementing the vision?
Action Framework/ Strategic Directions	• What clues tell you that the group is ready to move but that they just don't know how to get started? • What signs indicate that the group has spent time researching and studying and is ready for implementation?	• What specific, realistic, doable steps bring us closer to our vision and help us overcome our blocks? • What labels can you give each cluster of actions? • What three or four broad strategies are being suggested?
Accomplishment Phasing	• Has the group written up goals, concrete objectives, and specific actions, but does not know what to do first? • What signs reveal that the group may be so overwhelmed they are afraid to start anywhere?	• What events, projects, accomplishments, or happenings will bring about our goals and objectives? • How do we spread them out over the timeline? • What will symbolize the change we will have implemented by the end of this time?
Action Plan	• What reveals to you that the group knows what it wants to do but is blocked on the specific action steps to get it all done? • What tells you that the group has an easy time naming things to do and a hard time getting commitment to carry it all out?	• Project by project, what are the needed action steps that will guarantee the accomplishment of that project? • Who will see that steps are completed and by when?

Possible Uses

This tool is helpful when the contractor knows that a group has completed some work, but she doesn't know how much has been done or what stage the group is in. This tool can be used to review each stage in a group's journey and to ensure that the tasks of each stage are completed.

Practical Tool 4
Year's Accomplishment Chart

Description

The contractor uses this tool to help a group devise a year-long plan for visible achievements. Groups that have already determined their broad strategies can use this tool to project how and when to implement their strategies. The tool focuses on projects, events, or happenings, because these excite and motivate others about the task of school transformation.

Example

YEAR'S ACCOMPLISHMENT CHART				
	August–November	**November–January**	**February–April**	**April–June**
Centering on the Child	• Schoolwide author's chair • Assessment tools • All teachers greet children at door	• Schoolwide author's chair • Assessment tools • All teachers greet children at door • Class meetings once a week	• Schoolwide author's chair • Assessment tools • All teachers greet children at door • Stress cross-age tutoring	• Schoolwide author's chair • Assessment tools • All teachers greet children at door • Author's fair • Student project planning
Enhancing Staff Growth	• No negative talk in staff (25¢ honor jar) • Share effective volunteer use and grade level volunteer coordinator • Analyze curriculum, prioritize & delete, first by grade then by consensus	• Progressive dinner • Incorporate staff development (guest speaker)	• Create form listing staff interests, talents, resources (share strengths) • Exercise before/after school (staff and community)	• Rotating "Road Show"— a favorite activity you could share with school, room by room
Maximizing All Our Resources	• Curriculum night • Strengthen participation with PTO • Bulletin board • Homework Center	• Community open house • Development wish list • Parent liaison for press on kid stuff	• Coordinate incentives for fund raisers • Staff input with funds • Community newspaper	• Earth Day activity • Year end celebration with community • Community service

From: Raleigh Hills Elementary School, Beaverton, Oregon, August 1995

Instructions

1. Distribute copies of any planning tasks that have been accomplished so far—especially those that target broad strategies or major functions.

2. Create a Year's Accomplishment Chart in the front of the room with the broad strategies along the left side and time periods across the top.

3. Divide the group into teams and assign one strategy to each team. Allow time for individuals to come up with projects, events, or accomplishments that will implement their major strategy. Remind them to consider any material generated in the planning process so far.

4. Direct individuals to discuss their ideas with their teams. Ask each team to choose the best 8–12 ideas and write them onto 5" x 8" cards, one idea per card.

5. Ask teams to distribute their cards across the time periods on the chart, placing two or three projects in each time period.

6. Encourage each team to report on the projects and events they have planned. After each team reports, ask the group for any questions or comments.

7. Complete the chart and ask group members if the plan flows well through the year. Solicit the group to voice suggestions or concerns.

8. Lead the group to survey the entire display and note projects and events listed by one team that connect or support another team's suggestions. Some adjustments may be needed when looking at the whole picture so that projects can be coordinated to occur at the optimum time or so that they can have maximum impact.

9. Ask the group if they accept this plan and if they will carry out the plan in the next year. Modify the plan until the group accepts the plan and agrees to follow it.

10. Close the activity with few processing questions:

    a. What projects or events especially please you?

    b. Which projects or events are you looking forward to?

    c. Imagine it is one year from now when these projects have been successfully implemented. What new position will the school be in at that point?

Possible Uses

This tool is crucial for any planning process, because it coordinates the work of the school change teams. It allows the group to hear about a team's plans before they are implemented. The group can give teams the the go-ahead for their plans or they can voice concerns and objections that redirect the team. This planning can happen at the end of the school year before the staff disbands for the summer, or it can happen at the begining of year just before school begins.

Case Studies

Trusting the Process

A school district spent two years researching educational trends and visiting other schools. Five school teams studied different aspects of the school vision. A coordinating team comprised members of the visionary teams and members of the school board.

By the time the contractor (facilitator) arrived on the scene, many people felt as though nothing would ever happen. The contractor, over a 2 ½ day period held three-hour meetings with each of the study teams. In each meeting, she led the team to construct a practical vision, to name some possible underlying obstacles, and to develop a comprehensive action framework that would address the blocks and reach their vision. On the third day, she met with the coordinating team. The team reviewed all of the material from the five study teams and developed four strategies for the district. The strategies were to be sent to each school so that they might create implementation plans.

The three days of intense meetings moved the district from the research phase to the beginning of implementation. Cynicism was transformed into anticipation.

A school was directed to use a plan developed by a former principal and to create their own action framework and strategic focus. The school requested that a carpenter (facilitator) help guide them through this process.

The carpenter helped the group quickly to pull together their practical vision. The principal assumed that the carpenter would also help the group to summarize the blocks rather rapidly, but the group spent quite a bit of time discussing the blocks and related issues. What the principal thought would be a thirty-minute discussion turned into a painful, two-hour workshop.

At the end of that workshop, he told the carpenter that she had allowed the workshop to go on for too long. The carpenter explained that the group would not have been able to move to action planning until some of the blocks had been resolved; therefore, she allowed the group to discuss the blocks until they were able to name the real obstacles.

Indeed the action planning occured with lightning speed, and the group formed strategy teams to begin planning actual implementation. This was exactly where the principal wanted the group to be by the end of the day. The two hours on the blocks had settled some crucial issues and encouraged the group to move rapidly through the action planning steps.

IRI/SkyLight Training and Publishing, Inc.

Part 2

Skills
Trainer

Introduction

Whether refashioning classrooms, transforming instruction, altering the curriculum, working in teams, or making organizational decisions, group members embarking in school change need new skills (Fullan 1991). Unfortunately, few staff development programs provide training in the variety of complex skills needed to effect the school transformation (Fullan 1991). When process facilitators are designated, they often learn skills by the "catch-as-catch-can" method. Unfortunately, this method often fails, because it does not provide training in key areas such as building trust and rapport, making organizational diagnoses, building skill and confidence in others, using resources, dealing with the change process, and managing the work (Lieberman 1988).

The skills trainer steps in to equip educators with new skills. He willingly shares the secrets to successful facilitation. The skills trainer allows people to see what he does behind the scenes, so others can begin to do what he has done. He not only possesses the necessary skills, but he also discerns what skills educators need, teaches these skills, and carefully coaches educators to use their skills in their classrooms and throughout the school.

When we consider that school change involves three major arenas—the classroom, the staff, and the school—we can begin to understand the myriad new skills required. Increasing student learning and achievement calls for new instructional skills and strategies in the classroom and for teachers to cooperate in team teaching, lesson planning, and curriculum redesigning. Additionally, staff teams are being asked to participate in managing and restructuring the school. Skills training and retraining have become absolutely necessary for schools to transform.

If we expect dramatic changes in student learning and achievement, we must encourage dramatic shifts in adult learning and achievement (Fullan 1991). All levels and spheres of the school organization need to be involved in learning (Joyce, Wolf, and Calhoun 1993). School transformation cannot occur unless all participants acquire new skills (Fullan 1991). Educators have a right to demand that they be given enough time to focus energy on acquiring skills necessary to effect a total change. Leaders must understand that during skills acquisition, things may appear to be getting worse before they get better (Fullan 1991). Furthermore, when too little time is spent in skills acquisition, educators may believe that things have changed when they have not or when they have only changed on the surface. They have not acquired enough know-how to determine when real change is happening (Fullan 1991).

The skills trainer may assume three roles— the coach, the quarterback, or the sportscaster. The coach imparts to educators skills that can improve student learning and achievement. The quarterback passes on to educators collaborative skills that can promote shared decision-making. The sportscaster presents skills to teams to help them continually reflect and report on their victories.

Chapter 4

The Coach
Devises Strategies

The Coach is the Skills Trainer who focuses on student learning and achievement.

Role Description

The coach teaches educators new instructional strategies to enhance student learning and achievement. The coach takes cues from the class and individual students as to which strategies win in particular situations and which win with particular students. The coach utilizes Howard Gardner's insights on multiple intelligences to offer a variety of instructional approaches in order to draw forth and capitalize on the various intelligences inherent in each person.

Choosing Relevant Curriculum

Many books address the subject of curriculum, but one central principle emerges—curriculum must be connected with and relevant to the lives of students. Without this connection, students see no value in their learning (Astuto et al. 1994) and are not motivated to continue learning. Curriculum becomes useful only when it is relevant and meaningful to the students.

The coach knows that molding curriculum to students' needs requires teachers to adapt to new approaches and to acquire expanded skills. He

leads teachers to interact with students so that they can understand their students' concerns and can discern how to make curriculum relevant to their students' lives. When teachers create a dialogue with their students, curriculum moves from being a collection of dry, prepackaged facts to a dynamic and fluid material. The coach guides teachers to connect their expertise in content, the state's curriculum mandates, and the schoolwide curriculum with students' questions, issues, and struggles to mold lively, inclusive curriculum.

When teachers protest, claiming that they do not have enough time to cover content *and* consider students' needs, the coach emphasizes a "less is more" strategy. "One of the most often repeated slogans of today's reform effort in math and science asserts that 'less is more'—meaning that instead of mistakenly trying to incorporate all the new knowledge in these fields, schools should more thoroughly cover fewer topics, selected for their representation of the field" (Moffet 1994, p. 590). The coach leads teachers to move from deluging students with facts to teaching them themes, principles, relationships, and insights. Focusing on the larger perspective rather than on miniscule facts enables students to retain more and to connect the ideas and facts with their lives. "Authentic classroom tasks . . . prepare students for life, not just a test" (Burke 1994, p. xv).

Revising curriculum is an immense task; therefore, the coach guides teachers to form curriculum teams. Within teams, teachers divide up their work, offer suggestions to one another, and explain what has or has not been successful in their classrooms. Successful curriculum planning takes time, but this effort ultimately pays off. As students become more motivated, they learn more and present fewer discipline problems (Glasser 1990). "If students are actively involved in meaningful and interesting learning that allows them to simultaneously be challenged and feel successful, then the chances of students misbehaving are decreased" (Bennett and Rolheiser-Bennett 1992, p. 109).

Creating Collaborative Classrooms

Another step toward improving student learning and achievement is creating collaborative classrooms. Many of today's students come from unsupportive environments. Before learning can begin, the teacher needs to create a positive, supportive classroom environment. The coach trains teachers to create classroom environments that counteract the negative influences students face outside of school.

Research proves that cooperative learning strategies work (Slavin 1991). Cooperation enhances student learning and counteracts the negative influences students experience in their homes or communities (Astuto et al. 1994). "Teachers using cooperative interactions in the classroom say the positive effects on student motivation, achievement, and self-concept are so immediately visible and so astonishingly dramatic that the incentives are there for novices to do more" (Fogarty 1995, p. 208). When cooperative learning is done well, especially when it incorporates group goals and individual accountability, student achievement is notably increased (Slavin 1991).

The coach models how educators can promote collaborative classrooms by sharing their power. One method for sharing power is allowing students to work in small groups on clearly defined

and structured learning tasks. As students become accustomed to working in groups, the teacher asks them for suggestions about class guidelines and rules, for ideas about a unit emphasis, or for preferences for certain instructional strategies. Sharing power enables students to take ownership in their learning process. "Cooperative learning works well because through it students gain power. Lead-managers support this approach because they have discovered that the more they are able to empower workers, the harder they work" (Glasser 1990, p. 13). Imagine the motivation for students to learn when they experience a collaborative environment that is both caring and empowering.

Expanding Instructional Skills and Strategies

The judgment is in: Not everyone absorbs information by hearing a lecture; not everyone makes sense out of information through reading a book or an article. The richer the tapestry of instructional skills and strategies, the greater the chance of instruction reaching the widest number of people.

The coach seeks to train and model new instructional skills and strategies at every opportunity.

> Instructional Skills are usually discrete, less complex teacher behaviors that encourage students to learn. Examples of skills are clearly stating or determining an objective and purpose for a lesson; providing a link to students' past experiences; asking questions that actively involve all students; and responding to students' incorrect responses in a way that encourages them to continue thinking. Such instructional skills assist in the dissemination, processing, and retention of information, as well as increase the likelihood students will be involved in meaningful learning and will transfer that learning. (Bennett and Rolheiser-Bennett 1992, p. 110)

Instructional skills can be used in any teaching circumstance, with any grade level, and for any specific curriculum discipline. Most teachers learn these skills rather quickly but find it more difficult to learn new strategies.

Instructional Strategies are more sophisticated sequences of teacher behaviors. Strategies . . . have a coherent theoretical basis and provide theory-specific results. Their creators provide us with a rationale that explains the goals for which they were designed. When employed effectively, they help students increase their power as learners. (Bennett and Rolheiser-Bennett 1992, p. 111)

Instructional strategies include teaching approaches, systems, or comprehensive designs that are based on research and that have proven results. Some examples might include integrating the curriculum, teaching higher-order thinking skills, applying multiple intelligences theory, using multiage grouping, teaching for transfer, and creating authentic assessments (Fogarty 1995). Most teachers need time to learn, understand, practice, and incorporate these instructional strategies.

The coach not only teaches educators new skills and strategies, but he also helps them discern which skills and strategies to use in their classrooms. He encourages them to try different skills or strategies and to ask themselves these questions:

- Does it improve student learning?
- Does it engage students in the task of learning?
- Does it increase students' motivation to participate and become active learners?

The coach also explains that what may work in one classroom may not work in another, or what may have worked previously may not work this year. He encourages teachers to become skilled in many strategies, so when one idea does not work, they can try another.

The coach always reminds educators that the goal of employing any skill or strategy is to improve student learning and achievement. No instructional skill or strategy is a cure-all. If a teacher is to motivate students, he not only needs to use a variety of skills and strategies, but he also needs to choose strategies that enhance learning in particular lessons. If our classrooms are to become centers of dynamic thinking and

active learning, teachers need to implement a variety of instructional strategies (Bennett and Rolheiser-Bennett 1992).

Building a Supportive School Environment

The school environment can encourage or limit the willingness of a teacher to adapt curriculum, to create a cooperative classroom, or to adapt new skills and strategies. Teachers find it nearly impossible to create warm, dynamic, lively classroom environments when their school environment is autocratic and controlling. For example, some teachers hesitate to use new strategies in their classrooms for fear that their principals will unexpectedly drop by and wonder what is going on. When teachers operate under this fear, they tend to stick to tried and true approaches rather than experiment with new strategies. If a teacher is to experiment with new instructional strategies, then he needs support from administrators, principals, and other teachers.

The coach seeks to create a supportive school environment that promotes student learning and achievement. He encourages administrators and principals to participate in instructional training along with the faculty. Teachers cannot receive encouragement and guidance to experiment if the school administrator and principal do not know what the experimenting is about (Byham 1992).

The coach also encourages all educators to pursue action research—to try new research-supported ideas and to see how they work—in all areas of the school. "In self-renewing schools, the entire organization conducts action research, enabling teachers, schools, and the organization to study themselves as they make initiatives for the improvement of student learning" (Joyce, Wolf, and Calhoun 1993). Experimenting with new skills and strategies is not limited just to classrooms; all areas of the school can benefit from new approaches.

When This Role Is Needed

The coach adopts this role when he encounters educators who refuse to consider new approaches to teaching and learning. The coach steps in when discipline problems, absenteeism, and low grades indicate that teachers are not getting through to their students. Schools with high teacher turnover and low teacher morale need a coach who teaches them new strategies and skills and fosters a cooperative environment.

Skills

The coach teaches skills to educators that increase student learning and achievement. He is gifted in using and teaching many instructional strategies and approaches. His flexibility allows him to employ a new strategy or approach when it is needed. He can discern when a strategy fits a classroom situation and when it does not. The coach is also skilled in cooperative techniques and passes on these techniques to teachers and adminstrators.

Practical Tools

The coach can use the following practical tools to assist him in devising and teaching instructional strategies:

1. Curriculum-Instruction-Assessment Triangle
2. Cooperative Learning Lesson Plan
3. Three-Story Questions
4. Multiple Intelligences Unit Plan
5. Teacher Self-Examination Guide

Practical Tool 1
Curriculum-Instruction-Assessment Triangle

Description

A school change group can use the Curriculum-Instruction-Assessment Triangle to get a quick handle on what is going on in the classroom. It helps teachers see breakthroughs in the classroom and pulls together what teachers know about educational research. It gives the coach an instant view of what skills are already being used.

Example

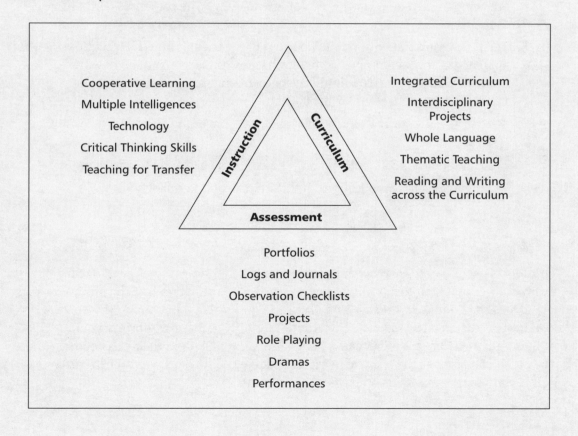

Instructions

1. Draw a triangle on a piece of chart paper or on a blank overhead. Label the right side "Curriculum," the left side "Instruction," and the bottom "Assessment."

2. Ask the group what new approaches are being implemented in the area of curriculum. Write responses on that side of the triangle.

3. Remind the group that changing data on one side of the triangle impacts the other two sides. (For example, if a teacher chooses to emphasize thinking skills in his curriculum, he begins to ask many more open-ended questions or assigns tasks that call for higher-order thinking. He also needs to use some method or tool for assessing these thinking skills. If a teacher chooses to use cooperative groupings in his instruction, he may elect to structure the curriculum based on the particular facets his groups showed interest in. In addition, he needs to structure the learning tasks so that he can discern what individual learning has occurred.)

4. Move to the other side of the triangle and ask the group what new approaches are being implemented in the area of instruction. Write responses on that side of the triangle.

5. Turn the group's attention to the bottom of the triangle and ask what new approaches are being implemented in the area of assessment and how the implementations in curriculum development and instruction impact assessment. Write responses under the bottom of the triangle.

6. Ask the group to review all the information on the triangle. Ask the following questions:

   a. How are teachers implementing these approaches in their classrooms?

   b. What are some implications of this information in our school?

Possible Uses

This tool is useful for groups that are meeting for the first time. If the coach (facilitator) has never met with the group, has never worked in a situation that the group is facing, or is beginning a workshop and is uncertain of where the group is, this tool can help him get an overview of where the group stands. By gathering information up front, group members are prepared to discuss what is going on in their classrooms. The coach can also use the triangle to expand middle and high school teachers' attention beyond their usual focus on curriculum content.

Practical Tool 2
Cooperative Learning
Lesson Plan

Description

Often, teachers cannot understand a concept or figure out how to translate a concept into classroom practice without the use of a concrete guide. The cooperative learning lesson plan is such a guide. (This tool is adapted from *Blueprints for Thinking in the Cooperative Classroom* by James Bellanca and Robin Fogarty [1991, p. 331].)

Example

COOPERATIVE LEARNING LESSON PLAN

Name _____   Grade, Subject _____

Lesson Objective	Hook	Roles	Materials for Students
Each group chooses a main idea sentence, writes 3–4 detail sentences, and concludes with an ending sentence to restate the main idea.	Review jigsaw—how each piece is important. Demonstrate 4 parts necessary to create a sandwich. Pass out parts made out of paper. Combine parts ot make a sandwich.	Organizer Encourager Recorder/reporter * Review tasks * Keep role cards nearby	Each group receives paste and a piece of colored construction paper **For Teacher** Awards

Room Configuration, Type of Group, Number in Each Group	Task Directions
Groups of 3	1. Encourager chooses main idea sentence from bag 2. Each person in group writes one sentence to support the main idea and puts it onto small piece of paper 3. Group decides on best order and brainstorms ending sentence 4. Reporter/recorder glues sentences in order onto construction paper. 5. Read paragraphs to class 6. Give awards 7. Hold processing conversation

(Continued on next page)

BUILD in Higher Order Thinking	**UNIFY** the Teams	**INSURE** Individual Accountability	**LOOK** Over and Discuss	**DEVELOP** Social Skills
Venn diagram Compare and contrast Building a sandwich Building a paragraph	Paragraph is pasted onto colored paper Awards for quietest team, teams completing task on time, and most cooperative team	Each individual writes one detail sentence for group paragraph	Questions for group discussion: What have we learned about writing paragraphs? What helped our group complete the task on time? What can we do next time to improve?	Stickers for using 6" voices and for saying encouraging words

Applications

Tomorrow everyone will write a paragraph on their own.

Instructions

Note: A blackline master of the Cooperative Learning Lesson Plan is provided in Appendix A, page 179.

Ideally, teacher teams can use this lesson plan in their curriculum planning. Individual teachers can also use the plan effectively in their own planning.

1. Instruct teachers to decide on the Lesson Objective, the Hook, the Roles Needed, the Materials required for Students and Teachers, the Room Configuration, Type of Group to be used, and the Number in Each Group.

2. Have teachers brainstorm the B-U-I-L-D contents one by one.

3. Ask teachers to create the entire lesson flow in the Task Directions section. The elements of the B-U-I-L-D section can be interwoven in the entire lesson flow.

4. Finally, have teachers write down what is going to happen next, where the lesson will go, or any further processing questions in the Applications section.

5. Lead the group through the following questions:

   a. What are some of the lessons you worked on?

   b. What was easy/difficult about this planning?

   c. What did you learn or realize about the process of planning a cooperative learning lesson?

Possible Uses

The coach can use this tool to lead teachers to develop cooperative lessons for their classrooms. This tool is especially helpful for teachers who are having a hard time understanding how to create a cooperative lesson.

Practical Tool 3
Three-Story Questions

Description

This tool acquaints teachers with higher-order thinking skills and teaches them how to ask higher-order questions. Using three-story questions can enable the teacher to connect information from the lesson with the students' lives.

Example

> ### Three-Story Intellect Questions for Watching a Video
>
> #### Three Story—Applying
> What if the hero had changed his mind earlier?
> How would you have ended this story?
> What could happen in the sequel?
> When have you felt this kind of tension and pressure? What helped you deal with it?
>
> #### Two Story—Processing
> Compare two characters.
> Why did the heroine do what she did?
> What messages is this video communicating?
> Compare this video with one we saw last week.
> What was the turning point in this story? Why?
>
> #### One Story—Gathering
> What scenes do you recall?
> What words or phrases do you remember?
> Who were the main characters?
> Who were the supporting characters?
> What objects were important?

Instructions

Note: Blackline masters of the Three-Story Questions 1 and 2 are provided in Appendix A, pages 180 and 181.

1. Explain the three types of questions using Three-Story Questions 2.

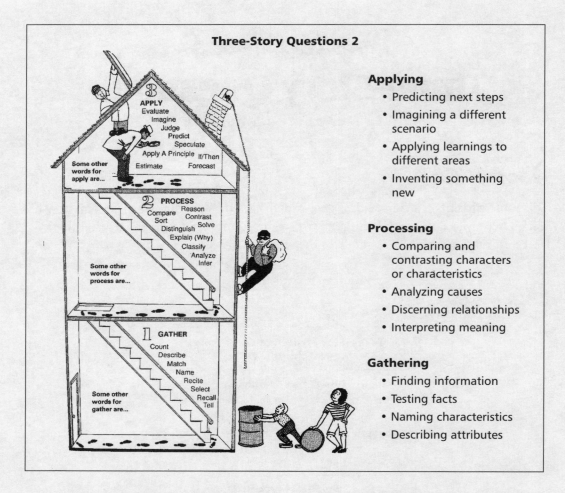

Three-Story Questions 2

Applying
- Predicting next steps
- Imagining a different scenario
- Applying learnings to different areas
- Inventing something new

Processing
- Comparing and contrasting characters or characteristics
- Analyzing causes
- Discerning relationships
- Interpreting meaning

Gathering
- Finding information
- Testing facts
- Naming characteristics
- Describing attributes

2. Direct teachers to choose a topic they plan to address in the near future and to spend ten to fifteen minutes thinking through the questions they could ask that would cover all three levels of the graph.

3. After each teacher has had a chance to prepare questions, ask for examples of questions from the first story. After each person has responded, ask other group members whether the proposed questions sound as if they would come from that level.

4. Repeat for the second and third stories. Be prepared to find that the third-story questions present the most difficulty.

5. Ask what insights they had about their own teaching methods after doing this activity.

Possible Uses

Questions organized along these lines begin to deal with in-depth thinking need to be included in each lesson. Constructing such questions may be strange to some teachers and very familiar to others.

Practical Tool 4
Multiple Intelligences Unit Plan

Description

Howard Gardner's multiple intelligences (MI) theory has helped many teachers break out of the habit of "monologic" teaching. Apart from being applicable to the entire learning process, MI theory can be used to plan an entire unit. When a teacher is constructing a two or three week unit plan, it is possible to incorporate lessons that appeal to many or all of the intelligences.

Example

Multiple Intelligences Unit Plan			
Logical/ Mathematical	**Visual/ Spatial**	**Verbal/ Linguistic**	**Interpersonal**
Graph the distances of planets from the Sun or from other planets Calculate how long it would take to get to the Moon traveling 100 miles per hour Classify planets by size and temperature	Draw a picture of what you think a Martian looks like Make a model of the solar system Make a clay sculpture of one of the planets	Develop a list of space vocabulary words Write a joke book for space creatures Write a short story set on a planet Keep a diary about a trip you took in space	Interview E.T. about his trip to Earth Role play the parts of each member of a space crew Plan a joint space expedition with Russia Practice peer mediation
Musical/ Rhythmic	**Intrapersonal**	**Bodily/ Kinesthetic**	**Naturalist**
Write a national anthem for one of the planets Write a planet rap song Create a new dance called the Space Walk Write poetry to the music from *2001 A Space Odyssey*	Meditate on being the first person to walk on the Moon Describe how it would feel to be the first student in space Tell how you would feel if you did not see sunlight for a long time	Act out man's first steps on the Moon Simulate the Sun or the orbits of all the planets Create a sport that would be popular in space (zero gravity)	Look for planets in the night sky Identify constellations of stars in the night sky

Instructions

Note: A blackline master of the Multiple Intelligences Unit Plan is provided in Appendix A, page 182.

1. Divide the group into grade level or department teams.

2. Distribute 3" x 3" Post-it notes and a Multiple Intelligences Unit Plan to each team.

3. Ask each team to choose a unit that would benefit most, if not all, of the teachers on the team.

4. Allow time for individuals to brainstorm various activities that can be used to teach the assigned unit. Ask individuals to list these activities on Post-it notes, one activity per note.

5. Direct individuals to place their activities on the team's Multiple Intelligences Unit Plan according to the dominant intelligence used for that activity. Have them put four to eight activities under each intelligence.

6. Direct teams to circle the three or four activities that best accomplish the learning goals and objectives for that unit and that use the most intelligences. Explain that they have just prioritized the most important activities for their unit.

7. Ask what they will do with the rest of the activities. (Some may say they can be saved for another unit. Others might suggest that these could become optional activities for volunteer projects.)

Possible Uses

This tool helps people break out of a single teaching strategy mode. Team thinking enhances the use of this plan because individual teachers have different combinations of multiple intelligences. Some teachers have even brought this planner to the classroom and have solicited additional input from the students for possible unit projects.

Practical Tool 5
Teacher Self-Examination Guide

Description

A facilitator led a group of teachers to create this tool. The teachers had been working on multiple intelligences, cooperative learning, and an integrated curriculum. The teachers created the guide to help the facilitator observe their classes. Groups can create a guide to evaluate their attempts at employing new skills and strategies.

Example

Criteria	Little	Some	A Lot
Multiple Intelligences			
Teacher Use	• Teacher directed learning • Limited visuals • Children working alone	• Teacher directed group work • Some visuals • Some movement	• Higher-order thinking skills • Teacher guided • Learning centers • Many manipulatives • Active experimental learning • Many visuals • Children working together
Student Use	• Teacher lecture • Student passive	• Some learning centers present—minimal use • Children hesitant to move	• Teacher as facilitator • Children using learning centers • Freedom of expression • Sharing of ideas
Cooperative Learning			
Cooperative/Social	• Much individual seatwork • Independent learning • Children raising hands, giving answers	• Working with a partner • Workshare • Lower-order thinking • Specific tasks	• Larger groups • Sharing everyone's ideas • Variety of cooperative approaches
Physical Configuration	• Desks in rows • Teacher desk in front	• Desks in rows, pushed together, facing forward	• Desks in groups of 3 or 4, teacher moving around • Teacher's desk hard to find

(Continued on next page)

IRI/SkyLight Training and Publishing, Inc.

Criteria	Little	Some	A Lot
Integrated Curriculum			
Overt Use/Relationships	• Language arts—reading aloud • No connections	• Incorporate language arts/social studies (novel/history) • 2–3 connections	• Language arts/math/science/novel/timeline/music/art scene from novel • 5–6 connections
Informal Connections	• Teacher/forced connections	• Some making connections/some not	• Students making connections/student directed
Students			
Mood	• Inattentive, bored socializing	• Attentive, occasional enthusiasm	• Enthusiastic, interested, active learning involved
Interaction	• Student/teacher interaction individual work	• Partner work	• Group work • Roles • Active involvement going beyond

From: St. Norbert's Elementary School, Northbrook, IL

Instructions

Note: A blackline master of the Teacher Self-Examination Guide is provided in Appendix A, page 183.

1. Ask the group to name strategies or skills that they received training in or that they worked on in the past few years, such as multiple intelligences, cooperative learning, and so forth. List these criteria down the left side of a blank guide displayed on an easel or a board.

2. Lead teams to break down these criteria into two or three elements. For example, multiple intelligences can break down into teacher use and student use. Divide the group into teams to work on each element.

3. Direct each team to develop indicators of progress—little, some, or a lot—for each element.

4. Have each team report on their guides.

5. Discuss the following questions:

    a. How can you use this self-examination guide?

    b. What did you learn as you created this self-examination guide?

Possible Uses

An administrator or principal could use this tool before he visits classrooms. Teachers schoolwide could create such a guide among themselves to indicate school efforts in particular areas. Individual teachers could create their own guides before a visit from an administrator to help guide the administrator's observations.

Case Studies

The Rubber Hits the Road

An elementary school elected to work with a coach (facilitator) over a three year period. The coach led several inservice sessions devoted to cooperative learning, multiple intelligences, and alternative assessments. In addition, the school staff implemented a comprehensive, schoolwide improvement plan. Gradually, teachers began to try new strategies and to implement changes in their classrooms.

The principal furthered the coach's efforts by encouraging teachers to transfer what they had learned in the inservices into their classrooms. He asked each teacher to turn in one lesson each week that used several intelligences. This ensured that over time all of the multiple intelligences were being represented in each class.

A teacher, encouraged by the coach and the principal, created a multiple intelligences unit on Egypt. She provided reading material, pictures, articles, and videos that featured Eqypt. After she and the class spent several days discussing Egypt, she took the class to a nearby museum that was featuring Egypt. When they returned to class, she asked the class to name connections between what they had seen in the museum and what they had been studying in class.

Another coach (facilitator) taught a course in cooperative learning over a several week period to a high school faculty. After several sessions, he asked teachers to bring back an artifact that demonstrated that they had used cooperative learning in their classrooms. He knew that when teachers see artifacts from other teachers, they can come up with new ideas for their classrooms.

At the next meeting, a Spanish teacher brought in an artifact of her unit on vocabulary of body parts. She asked students to outline a group member's body on a piece of chart paper and to label the various body parts in Spanish. This activity combined interpersonal, verbal/linguistic, and body/kinesthetic intelligences. She brought these pieces of chart paper to the next faculty training session.

Chapter 5

The Quarterback Leads the Team

The Quarterback is the Skills Trainer who focuses on shared decision-making.

Role Description

The quarterback leads the team into shared decision-making. She strengthens teams by demonstrating that their combined power is greater than the sum of each individual's power. She leads independent thinkers and doers into an identity of an interdependent force (Covey 1990). She fosters cohesiveness based on a clear vision of the team's task and each individual's role in carrying out the task. The quarterback increases team responsibility and accountability. She encourages teams to learn from their mistakes and failures, so they might transform them into victories.

Building Communities of Learners

As mentioned in chapter 4, collaboration is key to improving student learning and achievement. Likewise, the entire school environment can be dramatically altered when all stakeholders adopt a cooperative attitude and when all stakeholders know that they are part of a community of learners.

Our culture values competition, yet real educational change depends on cooperation.

Despite popular beliefs, competition may not create the most productive conditions for individual achievement. A counterargument is that self-motivation is sustained when individuals maintain a sense of self-efficacy and work in a context in which people (teachers, administrators, students, parents) help each other to develop skills, to take risks, and to challenge standard operating procedures. Competitive environments isolate people; cooperative environments bring people together and protect diversity of experience, preference, and interest. (Astuto et al. 1994, p. 53)

Real educational achievement arises from an environment of trust and support—a condition very difficult to create when competition is the driving value. When there is, for example, an overemphasis on standards and testing that increase competition, it can run counter to the collaboration that a school may be attempting to foster (Astuto et al. 1994). The complexity of the world, the expanding nature of information, and the rapid pace of change demand collaboration over competition. The quarterback's goal is to create a community of learners where students, teachers, administrators, community members, and parents work together to provide the best educational opportunities for all. She unifies the current school environment for the student who often lives in a fragmented, compartmentalized world. Students who arrive at school from violence-ridden communities and collapsed families often do not value learning. Creating communities of learners is one way to transform the confusing, helter-skelter worlds of many of our students.

Creating Stakeholder Teams

The quarterback promotes cooperation and creates communities of learners by forming teams. Teams can act as wedges, parting the old structures and allowing the new to move in. The current structure is often so rigid and the bureaucracy so entrenched that only collaborative effort and power can help the new break through (Maeroff 1993).

Traditional bureaucracies have thrived on solid and stable environments, but today's dynamic school systems are changing. Adaptiveness, responsiveness, and innovativeness are more crucial than ever before. This dynamic environment calls for flexible teams that build relationships in order to carry out work (Morgan 1986).

Advisory teams—teams that only suggest possible solutions—are not the answer. Advisory teams have often served to protect the hierarchical system, masking the truth that power still remained with the administrators (Astuto et al. 1994). The time for advisory teams has passed; it is now time for implementation teams to take over. Implementation teams have the power to make crucial decisions and the responsibility to carry out projects and plans. Implementation teams that encourage conversing, debating, problem-solving, and decision-making can transform schools.

The team is a powerful tool for school change. The team has power and perspective to transform resistances and obstacles. The team blends a variety of perspectives to determine what kind of change and which change tactics will succeed in the local situation. The team, unlike any individual acting alone, can bring about change across a whole school system.

If teams are the basic unit for getting the work of schools done, who does the quarterback recruit for those teams? The answer is anyone and everyone. The quarterback involves *all* stakeholders—students, parents, community members, businesspeople, teachers, and administrators—in creating and implementing school change. Partnerships involving school, family, and community are bottom line, but these partnerships require a constant flow of relevant information and opportunities for authentic participation. The quarterback employs a variety of skills to create and enhance communication and participation.

Schools have been isolated from their communities for too long. It is time for communities to share the responsibility for schools. Today's challenges require the support, creativity, and involvement of everyone.

> Returning schools to their public function means making families and communities co-owners in the schools. It means making democracy work through the process of sharing power, providing a democratic vision, and working collectively to create a multicultural and multiracial democracy. (Astuto et al. 1994, p. 31)

Teaching Team-Building Skills

Working in teams is foreign to most educators. Teachers are usually isolated in their work; therefore, they have little opportunity to work with colleagues. As this situation changes, teachers feel unequipped to participate in teams. Likewise, principals who have held the authority for many years hesitate at giving up their power to teams, and teams balk at making decisions that principals have traditionally made.

Teams cannot function if team members do not have basic team-building skills. Teams need to move from being a collection of individual talents to becoming a trained instrument in the change process. The quarterback spends time training all stakeholders to enhance their teaming skills.

> We will need to become savvy about how to build relationships, how to nurture growing, evolving things. All of us will need better skills in listening, communicating, and facilitating groups, because these are the talents that build strong relationships. It is well known that the era of

the rugged individual has been replaced by
the era of the team player. (Wheatley 1992,
p. 38)

The quarterback offers team-forming, problem-
solving, and collaborative decision-making skills.
She encourages teams to communicate with one
another and with administrators. She urges administrators to meet with teams and to encourage team decision-making (Byham 1992).

The quarterback has the skills and trust to
create teams that willingly take on responsibility,
decision-making, and action. "Carl Larson and
Frank LaFasto conclude that teams that succeed
have eight characteristics in common: 1) a clear,
elevating goal; 2) a results-driven structure; 3)
competent members; 4) a unified commitment;
5) a collaborative climate; 6) standards of excellence; 7) external support and recognition; and 8)
principled leadership" (Maeroff 1993, p. 515). The
quarterback teaches patience, knowing that teams
cannot emerge overnight when hierarchy and individualism previously ruled. The quarterback
models unwavering confidence that teams can
function more efficiently and effectively than individuals acting on their own.

At the moment, these instructional and team-
building skills often are not offered in teacher
education programs in colleges and universities.
But guiding schools today is infinitely more complex than even twenty or thirty years ago. The old
skills are not useless, but the new skills are crucial. The quarterback possesses these skills and
passes them on so that they can become a permanent part of the school's repertoire and skills bank.

When This Role Is Needed

This role is crucial when it is time to turn from
analyzing and planning to the actual stages of
implementation. When the group has had

opportunities for input and is clear on where it
wants to go, then it is time to create teams to par-
cel out the implementation tasks. The quarterback can also step in when an organization
decides to shift from a top-down, hierarchical
mode to a collaborative, team-building mode. The
quarterback can help teams shift from advising to
implementing. The quarterback also helps newly
formed teams to become stronger and more confident. She has abundant strategies to help a team
enhance its identity and its skills to work together.

Skills

The quarterback shares the tools and skills necessary for the team to become expert at shared decision-making. She possesses team-forming,
decision-making, problem-solving, and conflict-
managing skills and strategies for building successful teams. She is adept at creating safe,
nonthreatening environments that encourage everyone to get involved. She considers everyone's
contributions and solicits ideas from all stakeholders. Finally, the quarterback always models
collaboration rather than competition. She values
win-win solutions over approaches that divide the
group in any way.

Practical Tools

The quarterback can use the following practical
tools to assist her in building teams:

1. Role Assignments

2. Team Résumé

3. Valuing Differences

4. Team Attributes Conversation

5. Team Assessment Guide

Practical Tool 1
Role Assignments

Description

Team members usually assume several separate roles for the team to work smoothly. For newly-formed teams and for people not accustomed to working in teams, this tool can help team members discover the different roles they may have to play.

Example

The following are possible roles you may use with your teams. (The roles are adapted from *100 Ways to Build Teams* by Carol Scearce [1992, p. 67].)

Team Facilitator prepares the agenda and guides participants through it	**Recorder** writes minutes of the meeting for later distribution and files a copy in a Team Records folder	**Time Keeper** keeps the meeting on schedule as suggested by the team facilitator
Room Preparer/ Materials Gatherer gets the meeting space ready for the meeting and assembles any materials needed to conduct the meeting	**Spokesperson** reports the team's discussions and products to the entire group	**Questioner/Clarifier** poses questions to help the team think through its decisions and makes sure the team is clear on the issues being considered

Instructions

Listed below are four ways to assign roles for team meetings. You may choose to lead an initial conversation before assigning roles. The conversation might include these questions: What roles are generally important for us in our meetings? How shall we determine who does which roles?

Leader-Assigned Roles

1. Before the team convenes, the designated leader decides which roles are crucial for the success of the meeting.

2. The leader assigns these roles at the beginning of the meeting.

Leader-Suggested Role Volunteers

1. Before the team convenes, the designated leader decides which roles are crucial for the success of the meeting.

2. At the beginning of the meeting, the designated leader asks for volunteers to fill each role.

Team-Suggested Role Volunteers

1. At the beginning of the meeting, the designated leader explains the tasks to accomplish during the meeting.

2. The leader asks the team which roles are necessary for carrying out the meeting's tasks and requests that volunteers fill each role.

Rotating Roles

1. At the beginning of the meeting, the designated leader explains the tasks to accomplish within a few weeks.

2. The leader asks the team which roles are necessary to carry out these tasks.

3. Roles are rotated at each of the suceeding meetings.

Possible Uses

This can be a valuable tool if team members have difficulty working together. Sometimes, difficulties arise because a role was not filled or was carried out inappropriately. This tool also can help team members alternate roles so that teams do not stagnate and team members can try on new roles; although, take care to insure that roles are not alternated so often that members do not have a clear idea of a particular role's function.

Practical Tool 2
Team Résumé

Description

The quarterback uses this tool to bring the team together and to acknowledge each member's gifts and skills. This tool enables the team to lay out its own qualifications and to show the unique contributions it can make in accomplishing its assigned task. The team résumé also dramatizes the emerging group identity for the individual team members.

Example

My Résumé
Name: *Sonja Gomez*
Work Experience: *Kindergarten teacher, 2 yrs.*
Education/Professional Development: *Dual B.A. degree in education and music*
Skills/Expertise: *Piano accompanist*
Hobbies/Talents: *Snorkeling*

My Résumé
Name: *Shirley Vance*
Work Experience: *H.S. English teacher, 15 yrs. Assistant principal, 5 yrs. Principal, 5 yrs.*
Education/Professional Development: *Master's + 30, Administrative Certification*
Skills/Expertise: *Negotiation skills; head of teacher's union, 2 yrs.*
Hobbies/Talents: *Backpacking*

My Résumé
Name: *Hiroshi Sato*
Work Experience: *Middle school science teacher, 10 yrs.*
Education/Professional Development: *Master's in Science, Teacher of the Year Award*
Skills/Expertise: *Outdoor education; Chairperson of the Science Fair, 3 yrs.*
Hobbies/Talents: *Oil Painting*

Team Résumé
Work Experience: *27 yrs. of teaching (K–12) 10 yrs. in administration*
Education/Professional Development: *4 yrs. beyond Bachelor's degree, emphasis on excellence in teaching*
Skills/Expertise: *Artistic and outdoor experiences, negotiation expertise*
Hobbies/Talents: *Participation in activities to renew enthusiasm and vigor*

Instructions

Note: A blackline master of the My Résumé is provided in Appendix A, page 184.

1. Distribute copies of the résumé form to all team members. Give individuals a few minutes to to fill it out.

2. Guide teams to create a team résumé based on the contents of the individual résumés. The team can write the résumé on a piece of chart paper so that it may be displayed for all to see.

3. Ask each team to present its team résumé. (If many teams are present, ask each team to share one of the six parts of the résumé.)

4. Process the activity with the following reflective questions:

   a. What happened during the résumé preparation?

   b. What was easiest about composing the résumé? the hardest?

   c. What surprised you in composing the résumé?

   d. What did you discover about the members of your team?

Possible Uses

In a newly formed team, this tool can acquaint team members with one another. The quarterback can also use this tool when conflicts or disagreements emerge among team members. It can remind team members of their gifts, strengths, and differences, so they might work toward a harmonized solution. The résumé categories may be modified to fit a particular situation or stage in the life of the team. In fact, as the teams tasks shift, the contents of the résumé might shift to fit the demands of the new task.

Practical Tool 3
Valuing Differences

Description

Teamwork can be difficult when individuals feel they have nothing in common with other team members. These days, teams may include members with diverse perspectives and conflicting personalities. This tool reveals individual strengths and gifts and suggests that acknowledging the differences is the first step to bridging these differences. It is assumed that each perspective in the team has value and contributes to the successful operation of the team. (This tool is adapted from *More than 50 Ways to Build Team Consensus* by R. Bruce Williams [1993, pp. 211–214].)

Example

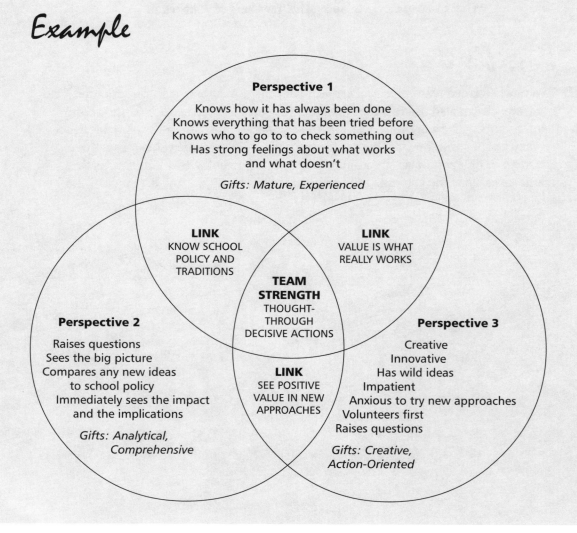

Perspective 1

Knows how it has always been done
Knows everything that has been tried before
Knows who to go to to check something out
Has strong feelings about what works
and what doesn't

Gifts: Mature, Experienced

LINK
KNOW SCHOOL
POLICY AND
TRADITIONS

LINK
VALUE IS WHAT
REALLY WORKS

**TEAM
STRENGTH**
THOUGHT-
THROUGH
DECISIVE ACTIONS

Perspective 2

Raises questions
Sees the big picture
Compares any new ideas
to school policy
Immediately sees the impact
and the implications

*Gifts: Analytical,
Comprehensive*

LINK
SEE POSITIVE
VALUE IN NEW
APPROACHES

Perspective 3

Creative
Innovative
Has wild ideas
Impatient
Anxious to try new approaches
Volunteers first
Raises questions

*Gifts: Creative,
Action-Oriented*

Instructions

1. Lead teams that have been struggling or have been engaged in conflict in a conversation about what has happened. Use the following questions or similiar questions to lead the group:

   a. What difficulties have been occurring lately?

   b. How does conflict usually emerge?

   c. How do we usually deal with our differences?

   d. What happens to our team effectiveness in these times?

2. Direct teams that have discovered that their difficulties stem from their differing perspectives or personalities to evaluate and discuss these difference.

3. Draw large interlocking circles to represent the varying perspectives of team members; draw as many circles as needed. Ask the group to use objective, nonjudgmental language to describe the related elements of each perspective within the appropriate circle. Write the information in the circles until each circle comprises one perspective and several descriptions.

4. Name the contributions or gifts offered by each perspective.

5. Ask the team to name ways that any two perspectives are connected. Do this until all possible links are made.

6. Turn to the intersection where all perspectives meet. Ask the team these questions:

   a. What does the intersection of all of the perspectives represent?

   b. What does the intersection suggest about the strengths of the team?

   Write answers in the intersection.

7. Process the activity with one or more of the following questions:

   a. What did you notice going on as we carried out this activity?

   b. What seemed to go smoothly for us? Where did we encounter difficulty or struggle?

   c. What happened to the team as we carried out this activity?

   d. How can this activity enable us to work with our differences?

Possible Uses

This tool calls for a great deal of team trust. Team members need to be willing to be forthright about what is going on with the team. The ideal time to use this tool is when team members are conscious of the presence of conflict but before conflict has a chance to erupt. It is helpful to follow up this activity with an informal, social gathering to defuse any lingering tensions.

Practical Tool 4
Team Attributes Conversation

Description

This tool helps teams define the qualities and attributes of an effective team. It also moves teams to devise actions that build these qualities and attributes. (This tool is adapted from *100 Ways to Build Teams* by Carol Scearce [1992, p. 113].)

Example

Qualities and Attributes	Special Actions
Cooperative Sharing Committed Focused Shares leadership Skilled listener Reflective Celebratory On-time Productive	• Hold monthly celebrations • Create rotating role assignments • Use journals to wrap up each meeting • Hold quarterly reviews of accomplishments and learnings • Create a team name

Instructions

1. Ask team members to recall an effective team they participated in. Guide individuals to draw a graphic representation of the effective team and its qualities and attributes.

2. Ask each person to describe their drawings and explain the qualities or attributes that made the team effective.

3. Write these attributes and qualities on the left side of a piece of chart paper. Direct team members to post their drawings on either side of the chart.

4. Ask for specific actions that the team might take to embody these attributes and qualities and write them on the right side of the chart paper.

5. Target several actions and discuss how they might be carried out.

6. Suggest that the team look at this list in a few weeks to see if there are more actions that they might like to try.

Possible Uses

This is an excellent tool to use with teams that have just formed and with those that have run into minor difficulties. The tool helps the team approach the difficulty as a team dysfunction rather than singling out a difficult team member. This is also a great activity for a team that is having trouble taking specific actions.

Practical Tool 5
Team Assessment Guide

Description

The quarterback uses this tool to determine how well the team is performing as a team. The categories can be modified or altered as the team grows. (The categories are based on the section headings from *More Than 50 Ways to Build Team Consensus* by R. Bruce Williams [1993].)

Example

CRITERIA	1	2	3	4
PURPOSEFUL VISION				
Overall Mission	Write and displayed	Refer to once a quarter	Connect to large team tasks	Verbally and visually connect to every team task
Specific Tasks	Some tasks seem mandated	Some tasks are overwhelming, others realistic	All tasks make sense	All tasks come from the group and connect to the overall mission
Documentation	Keep minutes	Keep quarterly plans and minutes	Keep and distribute quarterly plans and minutes to all	Keep and distribute quarterly plans, minutes, and meeting products to all
PARTICIPATIVE PROCESSES				
Leadership	Leadership works but never changes	Leadership highly effective but never shared	Effective leadership occasionally shared	Leadership rotated and information shared
Approaches	Sometimes one person controls	Input occasionally requested	Much input	Input directed and focused
Meetings	Start and end on time	Punctual; some tasks completed	Punctual; all tasks completed	Dynamic and punctual; all tasks completed

(Continued on next page)

CRITERIA	1	2	3	4
COLLABORATIVE TEAMS				
Working Relationships	Team members work with each other	Team members develop team cohesiveness	Team members support each other in tasks and differences	Team members take on each others' tasks when needed to complete team tasks
Roles	Individuals remain in the same roles	Roles rotated on a volunteer basis	Roles rotated according to a publicized plan	Roles rotated and periodically recreated and renamed
Recognitions/ Celebrations	Holiday parties	Birthday celebrations	Quarterly team victory celebrations	Frequent recognitions of team and individual accomplishments
INDIVIDUAL COMMITMENT				
Absence/Presence	More than 50% of the team present	More than 75% of the team present	Everyone usually present, some absences unexplained	Everyone usually present, every absence is explained
Attentiveness	Ten minutes to convene meeting, functions well afterward	Attention wanes after thirty minutes	Energy, attention high at beginning, decline by end of meeting	Members are alert and focused on the meeting or task
Dependability	Tasks assigned	Tasks assigned and performed	Tasks volunteered for and usually performed	Tasks volunteered for and performed with enthusiasm

Instructions

Note: A blackline master of the Team Assessment Guide is provided in Appendix A, page 185.

A facilitator, a team leader, or team members can use this guide to gauge team effectiveness. Teams may choose to assess their progress on a quarterly basis. They may also choose to create their own assessment guide with specific categories and indicators.

1. Ask the team to discern which stage of the first category they are in.
2. Brainstorm steps to help the team move to the next stage.
3. Repeat steps 1 and 2 for each of the four categories.

Possible Uses

The quarterback can use this tool to periodically gauge a team's progress. Team members can use this tool to judge for themselves how well they are doing. Teams can then discuss what they have learned about the team and how they can use the information gained from the guide. Teams may also use the tool periodically and review the guides so that they might note their journey over a period of time.

Case Study

Listening and Trusting

A school had been experiencing a general collapse of staff morale; conse-quently, staff members were backbiting, gossiping, forming cliques, and criticizing the principal's leadership. While the principal had many gifts, organization and administration were not among them.

The school called in a quarterback (facilitator) to lead some planning ses-sions. At one of the sessions, it came time to form teams and to choose who would be on those teams. The quarterback asked the group how they might assign team roles. Obviously, they did not trust the principal to designate team leadership. On the other hand, the group wanted to avoid voluntary designations; they feared that cliques would sign up together.

The quarterback let the discussion continue. Finally, an individual sug-gested that the quarterback pull names out of a hat and alternately assign the names to the implementation teams. The group agreed that this ap-proach made sense. The quarterback listened to and trusted the group; therefore, she led them to make a wise decision.

By chance the principal was placed on the public relations team—the principal's very strength. By chance, some strong teachers were placed on the site-based management team.

The management team quickly declared that all concerns or issues would be brought to their team for resolution. They explained that once the con-cern was voiced, the individual who mentioned the concern was to remain silent about it until the management team worked on it.

In a short time, the group demonstrated a deep commitment to operate as a team and to chart a new course out of the low staff morale. When she returned after several months, the quarterback found four well-functioning teams each encouraged and coached by the principal.

Chapter 6

The Sportscaster Announces the Game

The Sportscaster is the Skills Trainer who focuses on communicating visible achievements.

Role Description

The sportscaster ensures that educators continually reflect and report on their victories. He enables the team to extract meaning and direction from the implementation process. The sportscaster encourages "thinkers" to take on engaging projects and "doers" to participate in thought-out, focused action. He facilitates the sharing of information between leaders and staff and among implementation groups. He helps groups gain confidence by leading them into simple, targeted victories. When he discerns that they have gained confidence, he guides them into more complex plans. He promotes ownership of the implementation process, because he knows that ownership produces pride and a contagious desire to stay involved in the implementation process.

Sharing Knowledge

As school change teams shift from strategic plans to tactical actions, they must share information—what they know and what they learned in the process—with one another and with other stakeholders. Often, educators do not realize how much knowledge they possess. Since decisions traditionally come from higher up in the hierarchy, teachers are robbed of the opportunity to exercise their knowledge. The sportscaster teaches administrators and principals to share information with teachers and staff and encourages teachers and staff to share information with administrators and principals.

The sportscaster shares information before, during, and after the implementation phase. He wisely discerns what information is needed at which stage of the process. He talks with everyone involved in school change. He meets with teachers and leaders. He roams the halls and visits classrooms. He advises staff and leaders to consider research and proven methods (Byham, 1992).

The sportscaster insures that information flows among implementation teams as the process continues. He helps teams share their successes with one another and with interested stakeholders. He encourages teams to share what is working well and to ask for help from one another when it is needed.

Reflecting on the Process

The only way for groups to know that a research-based strategy or method is good for a particular educational situation is to try it.

> Acting should precede planning, Weick
> said, because it is only through action and

implementation that we create the environment. Until we put the environment in place, how can we formulate our thoughts and plans? . . . Abstract planning divorced from action becomes a cerebral activity of conjuring up a world that does not exist. (Wheatley 1992, p. 37)

Educational change is not a once and for all event; it is a gradual process, unfolding step by step. Fullan explains that change follows three phases: 1) "initiation, mobilization, or adoption"; 2) "implementation or initial use"; and 3) "continuation, incorporation, routinization, or institutionalization" (Fullan 1991). This unfolding allows school change groups to examine, experiment, and revise as they go along. Once plans are implemented, groups can evaluate how plans are working and how they might be modified to work better. They can decide whether to drop a plan that seems to be failing or to implement a school- or districtwide plan that seems to be succeeding. Even a seeming failure can be turned into a learning experience or a source for motivation (Byham 1992).

One of the most crucial aspects of the sportscaster's role is enabling people to reflect on what is happening, what it means, and what implications it has for the future. The sportscaster helps the group use insights from the implementation process to assist ongoing planning, implementing, and decision-making. With key questions, the sportscaster directs the group to hone and polish its actions by assessing what it learned from earlier implementation phases.

The sportscaster guides group discussion and individual reflection to help educators ascertain meaning from their situation. He sets aside time for individuals and groups to evaluate their actions. As implementers review their successes and failures, they become more involved and committed to their work.

Reflection allows school change participants to begin to revise their deep beliefs. "Most people do not discover new understanding until they have delved into something. In many cases, changes in behavior precede rather than follow changes in belief (Fullan 1985)" (Fullan 1991, p. 91). The shift from change in behavior to

change in belief can be enhanced through group discussion or individual reflection. Sometimes new insights arise when an individual spends time writing in a reflective journal. At other times, a new approach may suddenly make sense in the midst of a group workshop when someone explains an idea in a different way. The point is that individuals and groups need time to develop meaning in their pursuit of change. "The crux of change involves the development of meaning in relation to a new idea, program, reform, or set of activities. But it is *individuals* who have to develop new meaning" (Fullan 1991, p. 92).

Communicating Victories

The sportscaster skillfully keeps groups communicating about their victories. Many schools find their morale bogged down with increasing state mandates, falling standardized test scores, decreasing funding, discouraging home environments, and waning public opinion of education and educators. Many educators find it easier to talk about these major hurdles than to discuss even minor improvements.

What if a large percentage of the teachers' lounge conversations were devoted to the small successes and victories? Or, what if one-third of every faculty meeting were devoted to sharing strategies that were working in the classroom?

The sportscaster enables educators to move from discussing negative issues to proclaiming improvements. He uses communication strategies—group-discussion skills training, periodic implementation-review workshops, show and tells, videos, positive articles in the local press—to keep both the staff and the community focused on real victories. He guides the school to transform every dimension of communication to center on the victories. He may even encourage teams to post charts documenting victories—showing clearly what progress has been made and what else needs to happen (Byham 1992).

Communicating success can inspire others to become involved in the change process and to try new strategies in the classroom. It can also encourage teams to continue their hard work. An unceasing, external focus on the visible victories can have an internal impact on the morale and courage of the staff.

Promoting Ownership

The sportscaster allows the implementers to own the process and the victories. When implementers take full ownership, support and momentum grow, and colleagues volunteer to join in and help. "Driven by a common vision that has been fashioned through consensus, members of the team are to carry out their work in visible ways that implicitly invite colleagues to embrace the team's mission" (Maeroff 1993, p. 514).

A mood of collaboration and a willingness to share is so contagious that it can spread throughout an entire school (Byham 1992). As the news of successes permeates the school, teachers gain pride in their work and willingly share winning strategies. The enthusiasm can even spread to students; they may volunteer to help and to work alongside teachers to accomplish the school's mission (Byham 1992). The sportscaster encourages all stakeholders to take pride and ownership in the process of school change.

When This Role Is Needed

The sportscaster enables the group to target its first visible victories. He motivates the group to move from discussion to action. He rescues projects that have been bogged down, and he illuminates alternatives so implementation can continue. When a group completes a few simple victories, the sportscaster challenges the group to tackle more complex and comprehensive projects.

The sportscaster continually shines a spotlight on the next possible pathways of implementation.

Skills

The sportscaster assures that at the heart of visible victories is communication about what is happening in the school change process. The sportscaster shares any information that sheds light on the implementation process—information about what is needed to make sound implementation decisions; information about what is going on in implementation; information from federal, state, and district sources that would impact implementation; information about the public's response to the implementation. He has the ability to share data in a clear format so the group can discern ideas from the data. The sportscaster also can guage when a group has gained enough confidence to discern when it is ready to move to more complex projects. Finally, the sportscaster teaches the group how to celebrate and publicize victories.

Practical Tools

The sportscaster can use the following tools to assist him in helping teams communicate visible victories:

1. Five-Year Phasing Chart
2. Three Stages Chart
3. Balloons Victory Report
4. Implementation Learnings Discussion
5. Next Year's Award Ceremony

Practical Tool 1
Five-Year Phasing Chart

Description

The Five-Year Phasing Chart helps a group phase in a long-term plan, leaving room for fine-tuning or adjusting as new information is available. This tool is similar to, but more complex than, the Year's Accomplishment Chart featured in chapter 3 (tool 4).

Example

Five-Year Phasing Chart					
Years / **Strategic Directions**	**Year One**	**Year Two**	**Year Three**	**Year Four**	**Year Five**
Enhancing Student Achievement, Responsibility, and Learning	• Begin community service project pilots • Research new instructional strategies • Begin authentic assessment training	• Emphasize student learning goals • Start instructional strategies pilots • Receive intensive training in instructional strategies	• Initiate school-wide service project participation • Urge all teachers to use new instructional strategies • Begin team teaching pilots	• Begin yearly research projects with student teams • Start interdisciplinary curriculum pilot • Emphasize school beyond the school walls	• Compile student achievement, training, and documentation reports • Implement schoolwide interdisciplinary curriculum
Transforming the School System	• Receive training in team building/consensus • Visit schools that are restructuring or experimenting • Research block scheduling options	• Move to site-based management teams • Shift daily schedule • Immerse students and teachers in technology	• Initiate year-round schedule • Start technology course pilots • Push coordinated professional staff development	• Refurbish facilities • Open county-wide technology center • Become a showcase school for the entire state	• Begin international students network • District schools quarterly sharing events
Expanding Community Resources and Support	• Initiate business partnerships • Hire full-time grant writer/resource coordinator • Develop community resources handbook	• Expand student apprenticeships • Apply for grants in instruction/technology transfer • Create student/teacher speaker bureau	• Expand community involvement in site-based management teams • Acquire up-to-date technology • Survey community for input	• Initiate social services partnership • Expand senior citizen involvement • Begin community course pilot	• Open community social services center • Bring 2 or 3 adults from the community into each class • Initiate school as community learning center

IRI/SkyLight Training and Publishing, Inc.

Instructions

Note: A blackline master of the Five-Year Phasing Chart is provided in Appendix A, page 186.

1. Divide the group into strategy teams. Distribute a copy of the Five-Year Phasing Chart to each team member.

2. Ask teams to determine benchmarks that signify when strategies have been reached and to brainstorm various projects that could meet the goals of the strategies. (Give team members some guidance on what constitutes a concrete project. For example, "naming a committee" is not a project. Legitimate projects might include holding career nights, planning interdisciplinary units, arranging parent workshops, and sponsoring multicultural days.)

3. Direct teams to choose two or three projects for each year. Ask teams to write each project on a 5" x 8" card.

4. Prepare the front wall of the room with years listed across the top and team strategies down the left side.

5. Direct participants to post their cards on the wall chart. Remind them to allow for a progression of complexity.

6. Ask teams to report on their projects and to explain the progression they chose. Afterward, ask if other teams have any questions, reflections, or suggestions.

7. Lead a discussion with these questions:

   a. What connections exist among projects?

   b. What projects support each other?

   c. How well does the implementation flow?

   d. Does the flow make sense?

   e. How might your team capitalize on what other teams are doing?

8. Process this activity with the following questions:

   a. What do you think and feel about this kind of implementation planning?

   b. What was easy for your team? What was difficult?

   c. What message does this whole plan communicate?

   d. Where will our school be if these projects are completed?

   e. How will the community react when this plan is fully implemented?

Possible Uses

This tool can promote ownership of the change process. If only a few people have been involved up until this point, this tool can encourage others to get on board.

Practical Tool 2
Three Stages Chart

Description

This tool leads teams through a three-stage plan for change. Fullan (1991) describes three general phases to the change process—preparation, implementation, and continuation. Phase one, preparation, includes all the work leading up to the adoption of the plan. Phase two, implementation, includes strategies for implementing the plan or beginning a new project or strategy. Phase three, continuation, includes methods for reflecting on the plan. In phase three, a school may choose to discontinue the plan, modify the plan, or implement the plan throughout the school or district.

Example

Three Stages Chart		
Project: Block Scheduling		
Phase One: Preparation (Initiate, Mobilize, Adopt)	**Phase Two: Implementation** (Pilot)	**Phase Three: Continuation** (Incorporate, Institutionalize)
• Research • Train staff • Visit other schools that use block scheduling • Summarize block scheduling options • Put community PR on block scheduling • Put community/parent/ teacher focus groups on block scheduling • Involve students • Decide whether to adopt	• Train staff • Organize staff implementation team • Begin one-year pilot implementation plan • Direct staff teams to iron out glitches or issues • Evaluate midyear input from teachers, administrators, students, parents • Evaluate end-of-year evaluation input from teachers, administrators, students, parents	• Train staff • Study and pull together all the evaluation input • Evaluate year-end recommendations • Decide how to continue • Use evaluation input to modify the original model

Instructions

Note: A blackline master of the Three Stages Chart is provided in Appendix A, page 187.

1. Distribute a Three Stages Chart to each participant.

2. Divide the group into teams according to the number of specific changes being initiated or according to the number of parts in a single change initiative.

3. Explain the three stages: preparation, implementation, and continuation.

4. Direct individuals to brainstorm action steps for the preparation phase. Ask individuals to share their brainstorming with their teams. Ask teams to choose eight to ten action steps for this phase.

5. Repeat individual thinking and team brainstorming for the implementation and the continuation phases.

6. Direct teams to write their ideas on chart paper.

7. Ask teams to present their charts, to explain their phases, and to tell how much time they would spend on each phase. After each team presents, other teams may question, comment, or make recommendations.

8. Guide teams to work on a detailed action plan to carry out the first phase. (Give teams forty to sixty minutes if needed.)

9. Process this activity with the following questions:

   a. What happened during your team thinking and planning sessions?

   b. What was easy for your team? What was difficult?

   c. What is your team most pleased or excited about in your plan?

   d. How will this change affect the students? the staff? the administration? the parents? the community?

Possible Uses

This tool is extremely useful when focusing on a few clearly-defined changes. This tool is also helpful when the school has written an overall plan, but does not know how to implement specific changes or approaches. Groups find that focusing on these three simple categories improves their planning skills.

Practical Tool 3
Balloons Victory Report

Description

This tool allows the group to see visual representations of its accomplisments. By graphically representing each victory, project, or accomplishment, the group can discover and discuss what has already happened and what can happen next.

Examples

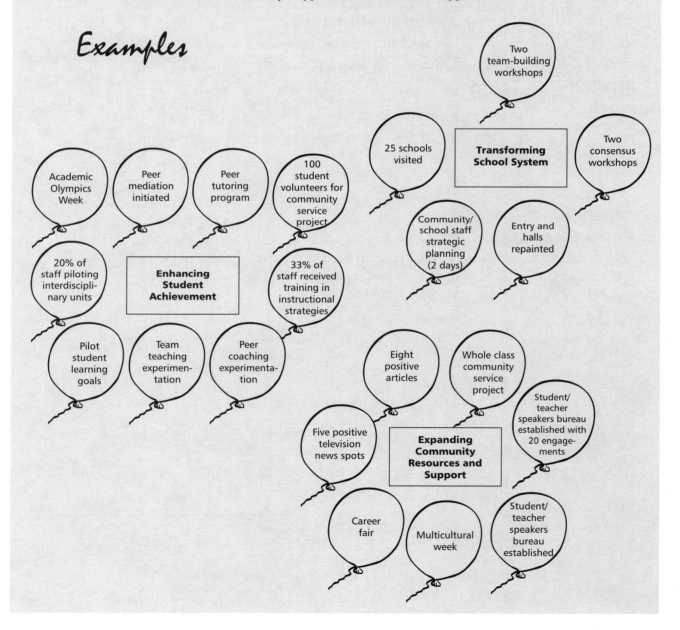

Instructions

Note: A blackline master for Balloons Victory Report is provided in Appendix A, page 188.

1. Direct teams to brainstorm victories, projects, or accomplishments that have happened in the past six months (or three months, year, etc.) that fit the team's strategies or emphases. Inform the teams that the accomplishments need not be restricted to just those that were identified during planning.

2. Pass out one 5" x 8" card and several copies of the Balloon Master to each team. Ask teams to write their team strategy or emphasis on the card and to write the names of each victory, project, or accomplishment on the balloons, one project per balloon.

3. Direct teams to tape their cards and completed balloons on the wall. (The card should be in the middle, surrounded by a circle of balloons.)

4. Conduct a conversation with the following questions:

   a. What accomplishments stand out?

   b. Which projects had you forgotten?

   c. Which achievements surprised you?

   d. Which impacted students the most?

   e. Which impacted the staff the most?

   f. Which impacted the community the most?

   g. Which were easily completed?

   h. Which were difficult to finish?

   i. What message is this arrangement of accomplishments communicating to us?

   j. What would be a good title for the wall arrangement?

5. Ask a volunteer to type up and distribute the information on the wall display. You may choose to photograph the display before you dismantle it.

Possible Uses

This activity can be used to wrap up every implementation stage. It may also be used to boost a group's mood or to examine a difficult project, because it can help refocus participants on the whole process and demonstrate how plans are progressing over the long haul.

Practical Tool 4
Implementation Learnings
Discussion

Description

The sportscaster uses this tool to help the group grasp the full meaning of their implementation. This tool helps the group reflect on what it is learning about how to implement activities, projects, and accomplishments.

Examples

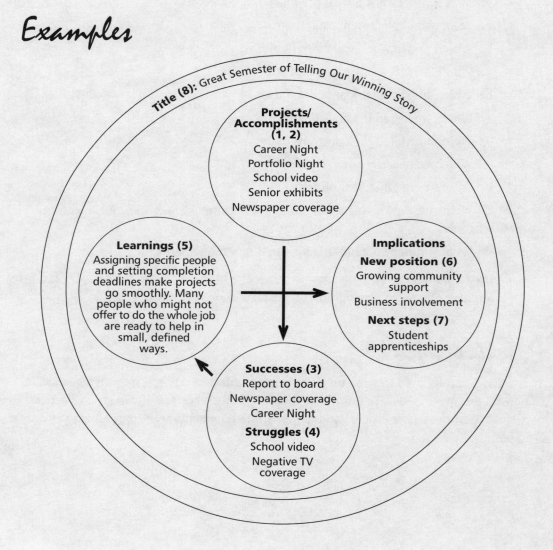

Instructions

Note: A blackline master of the Implementation Learnings Chart is provided in Appendix A, page 189.

Proceed from question to question, allowing several responses for each question. Many groups find the first two or three questions easy, but discover that more thought is required for the concluding questions. The facilitator or a team member may fill in answers on an Implementation Learnings Chart posted in the front of the room.

1. What projects in the past _____ (specify a time period) were most memorable?

2. What projects were most important for our team?

3. What projects went smoothly for our team?

4. Where did we experience struggles and difficulties?

5. What are we learning about the process of implementing our projects?

6. What new position are we now in because of our efforts?

7. How will our accomplishments affect what we do next?

8. What title might we give to this most recently completed period? (e.g., The Great Time of _____ or The Great Quarter of _____)

Possible Uses

This tool can be used after a period of implementation (such as a quarter or semester) to reflect and to set the stage for the next phase of implementation. It can be modified to process a project that went poorly to discover what can be learned from it. This structured discussion can be healing and can serve as a springboard for future action, creating motivation rather than discouragement.

Practical Tool 5
Next Year's Award Ceremony

Description

This tool enables the group to foresee the impact of future victories by imagining a future award ceremony. By enabling the group to imagine the future, the tool motivates the group to engage in serious planning or to celebrate the planning they already completed. (This tool is adapted from Marsha Caplan of M. Caplan Company, Boulder, Colorado.)

Examples

Instructions

1. Divide the group into implementation teams.

2. Suggest a specific future award for each team (e.g., Most Team Effort, Most Difficult Accomplishment, Accomplishment Providing the Most Positive Publicity, Accomplishment Generating the Most Community Support, Accomplishment Most Impacting the Students, etc.).

3. Ask teams to discuss the following questions:

   a. Describe the accomplishment that the award will be given for.

   b. What key steps are needed for this accomplishment?

   c. Who are the constituencies who will be involved or impacted by this project?

   d. What will the team discover about teamwork by completing this project?

4. Have each team create a graphic of their award.

5. Direct teams to explain their awards and to summarize their discussion of the questions in step 3. Acknowledge each team's report with applause.

6. Process this event with the following questions:

   a. What happened in your team during the discussion?

   b. What occurred to you as you heard the reports of these future accomplishments?

   c. What has changed in us because of these reports?

Possible Uses

If a group has undertaken little planning and seems apprehensive, this tool can give the group the courage to begin serious planning. Often, group members can clearly picture how projects can be completed after they work through this activity.

Case Study

Finding the Open Doors

A sportscaster (facilitator) was asked to work with a rural high school that was on a statewide watch list. Administrators and several teachers supported the change efforts as planning and training began. Within a year, many teachers were using new instructional strategies in their classrooms. Unfortunately, there still remained no real whole-school commitment for serious school change.

The sportscaster recognized that while intensive work in the high school was blocked for the moment, the district adminstrators supported extensive change. He led the leaders of the district through discussing and planning sessions. The leaders decided to spread planning and training across the entire district. The district sponsored teacher training in new instructional strategies. After one year, 20 percent of the county's teachers had participated in weekend courses to expand their instructional prowess, and two elementary schools had pulled together their whole staffs for planning and training processes.

Today, after this several-years-long, step-by-step change process, the county is known across the state as a "happening" place for education. Five years after the sportscaster began working with the high school, the entire district is participating in planning and training. The wise sportscaster patiently waited to find openings and he built on the successes and foundations of the past.

Part 3

Resource Consultant

Introduction

The resource consultant knows that school change requires a multitude of resources, and she believes that resources abound. She understands that others will share with schools when they believe schools have genuine needs. She is driven by the belief that "seeking assistance to solve complex problems is perceived as a source of strength and wisdom rather than as a sign of weakness" (Fullan 1991, p. 226).

Americans have abundant resources, but schools are often shortchanged because education is given a low priority. Thirteen of sixteen industrialized countries spend a higher percentage of per capita income on K–12 education than the United States (Astuto et al. 1994). State monies, the sole source of funding for most schools, have decreased over the past two decades; consequently, schools are forced to tighten their belts.

> Most American public schools are not bankrupt but struggle with budgetary levels that constrain conditions for improvement. Many schools work with a pittance for staff development, little or nothing for research and development, sharply limited funds to reassign teachers for curriculum or materials development, allocations that force the acceptance of assembly-line schedules at the high school level, and class sizes that block the development of teacher-student work teams. (Astuto et al. 1994, p. 17)

When schools ask for more money, people fear that the funds will be wasted or misused. Throwing resources into a situation does not guarantee that the resources will be used wisely or that the situation will improve. On the other hand, resources are often needed in the areas that are most often cut in times of budgetary restraint (e.g., staff training, art and music classes, etc.).

The resource consultant understands that resources alone neither improve a school situation nor guarantee school change. Yet she remains convinced that change cannot occur without an infusion of various assets (Goodlad 1994). Wisely applying resources can positively impact school change efforts (Astuto et al. 1994).

The resource consultant's mission is to convince the community that resources are needed and that they will be put to wise use. She guides educators to clearly define their goals, to explain why they chose these goals, and to predict how much money, time, and human resources are needed to reach those goals. She convinces educators to articulate their plans to the community, so that the community may take responsibility to meet the goals and supply necessary resources.

The resource consultant knows that just as other management decisions are moving to team decisions and consensus, resource allocation can be part of team planning and decision-making (Goldman and O'Shea 1990). The more the community is linked with the school, the more the community sees the school's needs. Then, the community becomes willing to share resources.

The resource consultant also creates support networks with other districts. She knows that all around the country, schools are dealing with resources in ingenious ways. She borrows ideas from other schools and applies them to her local situation.

The resource consultant intimately knows the local situation and focuses attention on precisely the appropriate resources needed to assist the local school. She searches out potential avenues to financial, human, technological, and material resources and puts these resources to good use.

The resource consultant may play the role of producer, director, or promoter. The producer organizes the project to benefit student learning and achievement. The director meets the challenges and overcomes obstacles through shared decision-making. The promoter advertises the successes.

The Producer Organizes the Project

The Producer is the Resource Consultant who focuses on student learning and achievement.

Role Description

The producer focuses first and foremost on gathering resources that improve student learning and achievement. She deftly connects school needs with human and material resources. While she is not necessarily an expert herself, she knows how to find and connect with experts who support and encourage teaching and learning. She also suggests materials that are realistic to the constraints of the particular school.

The producer is aware of how many resources are needed. She may know that the school has several needs (e.g., updating the physical facility, building a swimming pool, replacing old student desks), but she remains focused on the bottom-line task—enhancing student learning and achievement. She realizes that unless students show improved learning, the community perceives that resources are being wasted.

Battling the Scarcity Mindset

Many schools have heretofore relied on one source for support—the state. Yet state support has dwindled while demands on schools have

increased. Several educators feel victimized by this "do more with less" scenario and many develop a scarcity mentality.

The producer challenges this scarcity attitude with an attitude of abundance. She does not assume that no more state money equals no more resources, because she knows that other resources are available. Abundant resources—training expertise, community volunteers, business contributions, senior citizen expertise—reside within the community and within the school (Miles and Louis 1990). The producer takes the stance of abundance transforming the scarcity mentality into a generosity mentality. She convinces educators that they have the creativity and ingenuity to find resources within their schools and communities.

Empowering Resource-Gathering Teams

The producer stimulates teams and networks to seek and gather resources. She reminds teams that resource gathering is a permanent part of the transformed school (Miles and Louis 1990).

The producer teaches teams to articulate their needs. She reminds educators that the bottom-line task is to improve student learning and achievement. She convinces educators that this task is so vital that they need to become willing to relate their needs to those who can provide the resources.

The producer steers teams to discover alternative sources of income in the community. "'Going outside the frame' is crucial, not only in reworking existing resources in creative ways but in looking in odd places for what you need" (Miles and Louis 1990, p. 60). The producer sees the resource need as an opportunity to create more connections with the local community.

The producer also encourages teams to develop their own resources. She teaches them resource gathering skills, such as "how to broker the right assistance to needy parts of the improvement program; how to develop a clear contract with assistance providers, especially outsiders; and how to design and strengthen internal assistance capacity" (Miles and Louis 1990, p. 60). She reveals how thoughtful coordinating can multiply the total effect of available resources.

> Good assistance and coordination multiply resources through better decisions on other resources: staffing, time use, and educational practices and material. They also build internal assistance capacity. (Miles and Louis 1990, p. 59)

Creating Situations that Attract Resources

Schools that have lively discussions about learning and dynamic changes in student achievement attract additional resources (Goldman and O'Shea 1990). "But how do you create a dynamic situation without having resources in the first place?" an educator might ask. This resistance doesn't intimidate the producer, because she works through and around these resistances with clear vision and powerful teamwork.

> One of the biggest issues is facing up to the fact that changes cost money and confronting a second fact: powerful others may lack that realization—and may have to be persuaded . . . ., converted to supporters, or even bypassed. Finding and getting resources takes tenacity—hanging in there and persisting against obstacles. (Miles and Louis 1990, p. 59)

The producer starts small. She encourages teams to use their limited resources to set up demonstrations, pilot programs, and dramatic, creative events that improve and showcase student achievement. She enables teams to tell imaginative and powerful stories that generate interest and support. She teaches teams to communicate victories so that others will want to join the bandwagon of success.

When This Role Is Needed

The producer is needed early in the restructuring journey. Many educators operate with the scarcity mentality, so revealing resources may be a major challenge as soon as change efforts begin. The producer may also be needed when a team runs into its first snag—when the team needs money, an expert advisor, or more volunteers. Anytime a team feels it lacks resources, the producer steps in and connects the team to financial, human, material, and technological resources.

Skills

The producer connects the school or the district with the myriad resources located in the community. She understands and relates to the community and discerns obvious and hidden resources within it. She also knows how to amass resources from the region and the state to assist teachers in increasing their instructional prowess. She knows how to organize events that demonstrate student learning and spark excitement and support from the community. She uses flexible thinking to discover links between the school's needs and the available experts and resources.

Practical Tools

The producer can use the following practical tools to assist her in guiding teams to seek out and gather resources:

1. Source Location Chart

2. Community Resources Wheel

3. Eventfulness Star

4. Getting the Media on Your Side

Practical Tool 1
Source Location Chart

Description

This tool helps teams identify precisely what resources are needed to carry out a project and where those resources can be found. This tool forces teams to break away from their dependence on state support and to seek resources from other sources.

Example

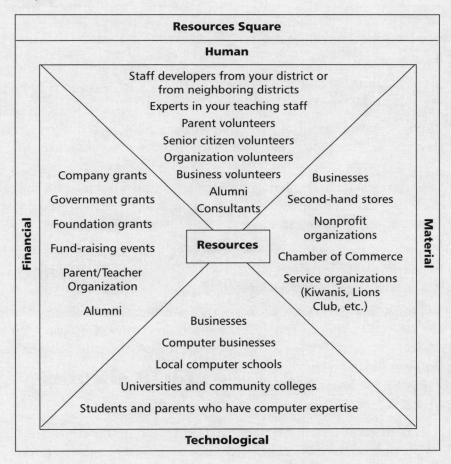

Source Location Chart				
Needs	**Potential Sources**	**Action Steps**		
		What	**When**	**Who**
Award ceremony prizes	K-mart Woolworth	Contact manager Contact manager	Jan. 10 Jan. 11	Mr. Soloman Ms. Jankowski
Videotape to record award ceremony	Blockbuster Target	Contact manager Contact manager	Jan. 11 Jan. 12	Mr. Johnson Ms. Cohen
Speaker for class studying Industrial Revolution	Tool and die plant Ford plant	Contact manager Contact manager	Jan. 9 Jan. 9	Mr. Kameyama Mrs. Sherry
Used computers	National Family Insurance	Contact CEO	Jan. 20 (meeting at company)	Principal and Mr. Chavez
Student apprenticeships	Chamber of Commerce Lions Club Kiwanis	Meeting presentation Meeting presentation Meeting presentation	Feb. 5 Feb. 13 Feb. 24	District superintendent and student Principal and student Principal and student

Instructions

Note: Blackline masters of the Resources Square and the Source Location Chart are provided in Appendix A, pages 190 and 191.

1. Display or provide copies of the Resources Square. This graphic helps a group expand its understanding of the available resources in a community. The group may write in any additional resources.

2. Divide the group into program implementation teams and pass out copies of the Source Location Chart. (If the focus is one major project, break the program into components and assign teams to different components.)

3. Ask teams to brainstorm what they need to make the program (or program component) succeed. (Teams may wish to consult the Resources Square.)

4. Brainstorm potential sources for each of the needs.

5. Build an action plan (what, when, who) for obtaining the resources. (Community representatives can be of great assistance in gathering resources. Encourage teams to recruit community representatives to help in this massive task.)

Possible Uses

This tool can be useful at the beginning of school change when the school and the community are unaccustomed to seeking resources. This tool can also be implemented when a budget cut forces schools to look elsewhere for resources. As teams successfully connect with resource providers, they gain confidence in approaching outside sources for resources.

Practical Tool 2
Community Resources Wheel

Description

This Community Resources Wheel provides a comprehensive six-step process to amass the resources necessary to carry out a program emphasis. The tool also provides questions to spark thinking in each of the six steps. (These six categories are adapted from *Preparing Collaborative Leaders: A Facilitator's Guide* by Wendy Russell [1994, attachment 15.2].)

Example

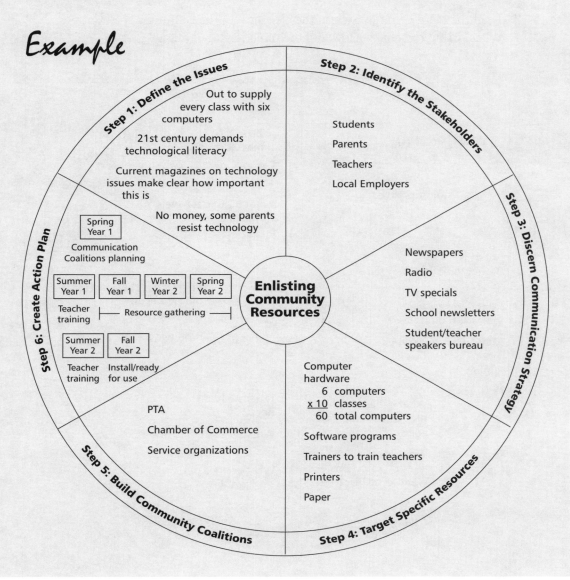

Instructions

Note: A blackline master of the Community Resources Wheel is provided in Appendix A, page 192.

1. Explain the six underlying assumptions for using this tool:

   a. Schools cannot do the job alone.

   b. Schools need the community.

   c. The community needs the schools.

   d. Open communication among all stakeholders is crucial.

   e. Resources are available in the community.

   f. Community organizations can assist schools when they are included in discussing and planning school change.

2. Lead the team through each of the six steps on the Community Resources Wheel using the chart below and the directions that follow.

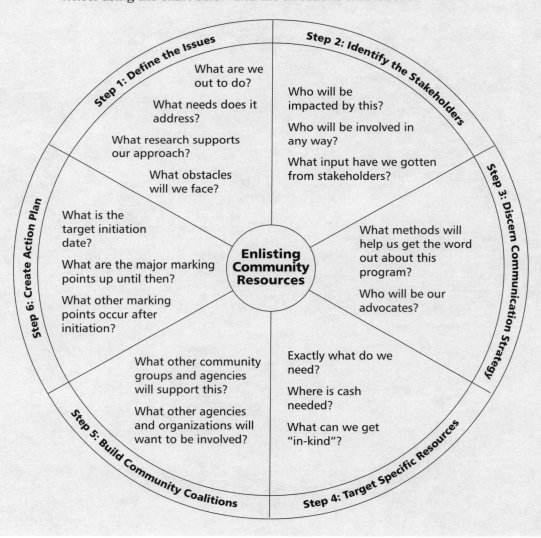

a. Step One: Define the Issues

Define the issue, clearly articulating what the major direction is. Present the definition and the overall plan in a clear, concise, readable format.

b. Step Two: Identify the Stakeholders

Initiate dialogue with the primary stakeholders, acquiring their input at every step of the way. The major direction must flow naturally and obviously from the stakeholders' input.

c. Step Three: Discern Communication Strategy

Communicate your plan to the wider community. Discern what channels of communication are available and suitable for your area (e.g., local newspapers, television, school newsletters, etc.).

d. Step Four: Target Specific Resources

Prepare a detailed and honest list of what is actually needed to initiate the program. Be sure to include everything that is needed without diverting into extraneous wants. Decide which needs can be fulfilled with available monies and which needs require community assistance.

e. Step Five: Build Community Coalitions

Approach community organizations, social clubs, and agencies that can either supply resources or can lead the team to resources.

f. Step Six: Create Action Plans

Lay out a timeline and break up the plan into large time periods. Articulate detailed plans—including what happens, who makes it happen, and when it happens—for the first two time periods. Schedule progress meetings that bring the team together to celebrate successes.

Possible Uses

This tool is particularly useful for groups that have never undertaken detailed planning or are not accustomed to carrying out action plans. Teams that are not used to working in coalitions also benefit from using this tool.

Practical Tool 3
Eventfulness Star

Description

This tool helps a group whose purpose is to gather resources or to involve the community in brainstorming a special event.

Example

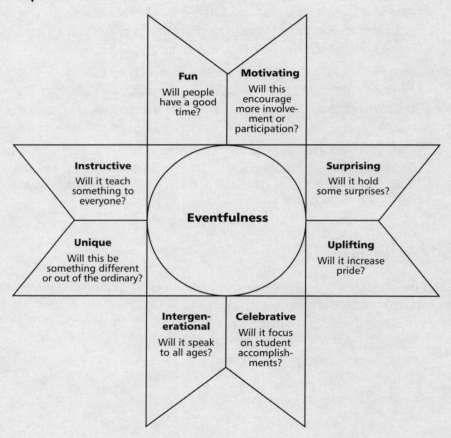

Instructions

Note: A blackline master of the Eventfulness Star is provided in Appendix A, page 193.

1. Gather 5" x 8" cards, masking tape, and magic markers.

2. Help the group decide what the real intent of the event is going to be (e.g., fund-raising, career exploration, student project display, etc.).

3. Ask the group to decide what they want participants to experience as they participate in this event (e.g., pleased, proud, excited, surprised, etc.).

4. Challenge individuals to brainstorm possible events. (If they get stuck, they may consult the following list for ideas).

Special Events List

- School Spirit Book
- Monte Carlo Night
- Railroad Days Event
- Family Dinner
- Fashion Show
- "Jumping Pumpkin" Event
- Student Art Exhibit

- Gourmet Food Sampling
- "Winter Fest"
- Hall of Fame Dinner
- Theater Party
- Adult Spelling Bee
- "Mr. Betty Crocker" Contest

- Game Show Night
- International Night
- Senior Prom for Senior Citizens
- Carnival Time
- History Walk Through Town

---

5. Divide participants into teams of two or three. Instruct each team to choose the best three or four events and write the events on 5" x 8" cards (one event per card).

6. Direct teams to tape their cards to the front wall, clustering cards that are similar.

7. Challenge the large group to choose the best event from each cluster and apply it to the Eventfulness Star to discern which event meets the most criteria.

8. Come to final agreement on the best event.

9. Ask the group to return to teams. Instruct teams to write a short paragraph describing the event or to draw a picture depicting the event.

10. Ask teams to show their pictures or read their paragraphs. Ask the group to call out what descriptions they see and hear about this event and record these observations.

11. Divide into planning teams to initiate the planning for this event.

Possible Uses

A special event can be created to introduce a shift or a change in the school focus or instructional program. Special events can marshal community support or involvement and improve the community's perception of the entire educational program. Special events can also be used to raise money or gather other resources.

Practical Tool 4
Getting the Media on Your Side

Description

This tool enables a group to plan a comprehensive media strategy that attracts resources and improves the school's image. Positive reports in the media tremendously enhance any school change effort.

Examples

Getting the Media on Your Side				
Keep the Focus on Learning Victories	**Create a Dramatic and Informative Story**	**Plan Proactive Media Contact**	**Establish Personal Media Relationships**	**Expand Your Sphere of Influence**
Conduct student and teacher research and tell the media	Create a case for support and tell the media	Produce and host a cable show	Establish a media bank	Submit articles to professional journals and magazines
	Establish a profile	Conduct a media tour of your school and/or district	Recruit media professionals on boards or work teams	
Have *students* involved in your story—they are what it's all about	Talk about your *needs* and tell them about your *deeds*	Hold press conference for teacher/student accomplishments	Get to know your local reporters	Share your stories with other schools
	Create your own story		Answer every editiorial that is written about you	
	Prepare for all interviews, know your "stuff"	Create a media event	Ask media for student apprenticeships	
Celebrate any *wins*, athletic or academic	Send regular updates of your progress to all media contacts	Recognize media contribution (e.g., a plaque)	Follow up every press release with a personal phone call	Have a news clipping service
		Be proactive, not reactive		
Have *real people* involved in your story	Be optimistic, enthusiastic, informative, and honest	Have a photographer at every event	Reciprocate any media gesture with a thank you or flowers	Dare to be different
	Tell your story with passion	Invite all media to every event	Put media friends on holiday card lists	

Adapted from Allan Holender, president of Educational Fundraising, Inc., Richmond, British Columbia.

Instructions

Note: Blackline masters of Getting the Media on Your Side and Helpful Hints for Media Contacts are provided in Appendix A, pages 194 and 195.

1. Divide your group into five teams. (You may choose to remain in a large group and brainstorm columns one by one.)

2. Give each team a Getting the Media on Your Side chart. Direct teams to brainstorm two or three realistic and doable ideas in each column.

3. Reassemble the group and review all of the brainstormed ideas. Ask the group to share any additions, comments, questions, or concerns.

4. Assign individuals or teams to carry out these ideas. Encourage them to consult the Helpful Hints as needed. Set completion dates for each step.

Helpful Hints for Media Contacts

- Don't expect your interview with the media to turn out the way you said it.

- Don't embellish your story. Just answer the question factually as presented and nothing more.

- Don't expect the media to be interested in everything you're doing.

- Don't be discouraged if they don't use what you gave them.

- Don't allow yourself to be interviewed unless you know what the specific questions will be.

- Don't be surprised if you are asked unexpected questions; expect the best, but prepare for the worst.

- Don't talk about other people; represent yourself only.

- Don't anger the media. They will come back to haunt you and haunt you and haunt you.

Adapted from Allan Holender, president of Educational Fundraising, Inc., Richmond, British Columbia.

---

5. Arrange a date and a time for a follow-up meeting.

Note: The Getting the Media on Your Side example provides some suggestions for how you might go about getting the media on your side. You may decide to implement one or two ideas from each column. Pick and choose which methods will work best in your situation.

Possible Uses

Building a comprehensive media strategy is especially important for teams engaged in new approaches or when a school has received negative publicity. On the surface, spending time on publicity may seem to be a waste, but it is a wise investment if the community becomes more connected and involved in the school.

Case Studies

Making the Community an Offer it Can't Refuse

A small rural school district decided to transform its junior high/high school into a middle school and to move the high school into a new building. The newly named principal of the middle school was faced with the huge job of transforming a former junior high/high school facility into a middle school facility. Needless to say, cash was strapped.

Instead of focusing on the scarcity of cash, she chose to be a wise producer and looked for other resources to meet her needs. She went everywhere in the community asking for help. She got donations of paint and painting tools from the local hardware store. Community members loaned tools for minor repair work. Parents and community people donated time to fix up the facility, performing tasks such as stripping, mopping, and sweeping the floors; repairing desks; and replacing and repairing windows. The principal even got a group of female prisoners released to help paint the building and create an attractive mural near the front entrance. Local restaurants and fast food chains donated food to keep the volunteers working. A transformed middle school opened up on time.

A school district knew that its teachers needed a great deal of training and retraining to keep up with the challenges of teaching. Instead of sending every teacher to outside training, they decided to train a cadre of teachers to train the rest of the teachers.

The district created a twenty-member teachers' cadre by pulling volunteer representatives from each school in the district. The cadre received a four-day training on adult learning, presentation skills, facilitation skills, and peer coaching. Most of the cadre were sent to summer workshops on specific topics such as multiple intelligences or authentic assessment.

The representatives from each school organized presentations for their faculties on what they had learned. When the district offered an institute day for its enire staff, fifteen of the twenty cadre members led workshops for their colleagues. This district created a structured way to take the training given to a few and multiply its affect to most of their teachers.

Chapter 8

The Director Overcomes Obstacles

The Director is the Resource Consultant who focuses on shared decision-making.

Role Description

Any team engaged in school transformation encounters challenging obstacles. The director helps teams overcome strategy and resource obstacles. He ensures that teams pay attention to the obstacles so that their plans and actions are not naive or unrealistic. The director guides teams to identify potential obstacles, to see beyond surface irritations, to work through major problems, and to learn from the process of removing obstacles.

Facing Obstacles Head-on

Any serious transformation effort runs into obstacles. The director addresses obstacles head-on, because he knows obstacles do not disappear on their own. "Unless you analyze and remove the obstacles, education reform is impossible" (Moffett 1994, p. 590). In fact, the presence of obstacles confirms that reform is necessary.

From the start, the director encourages teams to develop plans that take obstacles into account. Teams that believe obstacles disappear by themselves, or that refuse to admit obstacles exist, insure the failure of an otherwise sound plan. The director advises teams to develop plans that comprise elements intended to bring about the vision of a school as well as elements intended to overcome potential obstacles.

Addressing the True Obstacle

Frivolous issues, concerns, and obstacles can hamper teams. The director enables teams to uncover core obstacles and to avoid dealing with superfluous issues.

> We . . . create order when we invite conflicts and contradictions to rise to the surface, when we search them out, highlight them, even allowing them to grow large and worrisome. We need to support people in the hunt for unsettling or disconfirming information, and provide them with the resources of time, colleagues, and opportunities for processing the information. (Wheatley 1992, p. 116)

Investing time in identifying major obstacles actually saves time down the road. The director helps teams to separate core obstacles from surface obstacles, to distiguish concrete obstacles from illusory obstacles, and to identify systemic obstacles.

Core vs. Surface Obstacles

The director looks beneath the surface to address the real obstacle. One of the cues that people are not addressing the core obstacle is the phrase "lack of"—lack of time, lack of money, lack of commitment, or lack of people. The director pushes the team to identify and address the real obstacles behind the perceived lack of resources. For example, the director and the team may examine the surface obstacles of lack of time or resources and discover that the core obstacles are a rigid, inflexible schedule or a budget set by outdated priorities.

Working with a team to identify genuine obstacles takes time and effort. Openly discussing obstacles may elicit bitter memories of failures and disappointments. On the other hand, many people are relieved when an overwhelming list of forty to fifty surface obstacles is condensed into five or ten underlying obstacles.

Concrete vs. Illusory Obstacles

Not only are there core obstacles as opposed to surface obstacles, but there are also concrete obstacles as opposed to illusory obstacles (Goodlad 1994). Illusory obstacles are articulated by those most threatened by the suggestions for change and improvement. For example, some teachers may claim that they will lose control in their classrooms if they adopt alternative teaching strategies. They may sincerely believe that loss of control is the real obstacle, when the real obstacle is their belief that they can only control their classes when they use the lecture approach.

The director addresses illusory obstacles very carefully. He knows that directly attacking an illusory obstacle alienates the person who perceived the obstacle or pushes them to cling to another illusory obstacle. The director channels the team's energy and thinking to identify the concrete obstacle beneath the illusory obstacle.

Systemic Obstacles

The director also looks for systemic obstacles, encouraging teams to question their assumptions about obstacles and their causes. How a problem is stated can reveal the potential for a solution or the certainty of solution failure (Morgan 1986). If obstacles are phrased systemically, the team can grapple with how to change the system rather than how to get rid of certain people (including certain students!). "Put simply, ... since problems may be a natural consequence of the logic of the system in which they are found, we may be able to deal with the problems only by restructuring the logic" (Morgan 1986, pp. 270–71).

For example, a school administration team was deeply discouraged by what they perceived as faculty ineptitude. They continually discussed their struggles to improve teaching. On the other hand, the faculty complained that the administrators were not supportive and encouraging. They had experienced closed doors and restricted communication with the administration. Neither administrators nor teachers understood the underlying obstacle. When the two sides worked together toward a solution, they discovered the underlying problem—neither group had articulated their vision for their school and their classrooms. That unarticulated, unfocused vision had become a schoolwide systemic obstacle.

The director encourages teams to focus not only on the obstacle, but also on the system the obstacle comes out of. He reminds teams that "many organizational problems are imbedded in our thinking" (Morgan 1986, p. 335). He leads groups to question their assumptions about an obstacle. He suggests that systemic reorganization or change may eliminate the obstacle or nullify its effects.

Whether obstacles are surface or core, illusory or concrete, or systemic, the director knows that naming obstacles is the first step in gaining control over them. "One essential skill is the ability to locate and state problems as natural, even helpful occurrences ('Problems are our friends') without blaming anyone, arousing defensiveness, or implying a predetermined solution" (Miles and Louis 1990, p. 60). Obstacles can reveal where we need to move, rather than prevent us from moving.

Enabling Teams to Challenge Obstacles

Overcoming obstacles requires more energy and creativity than one person can offer. "Team building is seen as a possible way to sidestep the institutional resistance to change that invariably greets the lone practitioner bent on reform" (Maeroff 1993, p. 515). Very often, the imagination and creativity of a team can challenge resistances in a way an individual cannot. Teams can provide the nurture and the support to sustain the effort beyond which an individual might burn out or give in.

> Against the united Zapp! of a team, the dragons [obstacles] had no chance. By working steadily to improve the quality of instruction and overall teacher and students satisfaction, the Zapp! Teams were giving them no food. So the dragons could not grow. (Byham 1992, p. 198)

Team power has more chance of "covering the bases" so that an obstacle has less chance to grow. The combined wisdom of the team can determine when to advance, when to stand back, when to challenge, and when to move on. Teams can transform seemingly impossible, overwhelming, and never-ending tasks into planned, shared, and focused accomplishments.

Reflecting on the Process

The director continually encourages teams to reflect on the process of removing obstacles. He knows that teams can learn a great deal from the insights gained in removing obstacles. "Reviewing recent problems, what was done about them, and whether they stayed solved can be illuminating" (Miles and Louis 1990, p. 60).

The director understands that teams are constantly learning as they tackle obstacles. Sharing and keeping tabs on that learning can dramatically increase the effectiveness of removing obstacles.

The director sets aside time for a team to reflect on what they have learned as they tackle obstacles. Reflection often emboldens the team to take dramatic and radical leaps in removing obstacles. The director encourages team members to think outside the normal frameworks, indeed to "break the mold." He encourages team members to share their perspectives, to connect their perspectives in new ways, and to imagine novel

strategies. The director also uses the reflection time to move educators from focusing on daily "firefighting" crises to projecting and solving problems before they become crises. He allows teams to perceive and eliminate future obstacles.

When This Role Is Needed

The facilitator shifts into this role when a team runs headlong into an overwhelming obstacle. The team may be facing resistance or it may feel that it has no options left. The director also helps the team when it is on the verge of giving up or when it seees no options for moving ahead. The director steps in when the team cannot grasp the big picture or find a way through the obstacle.

Skills

The director enables a team to work around, through, and beneath obstacles so that the team stays focused and functioning. The director does not remove the obstacles; he empowers the team to do so. The director helps the team clarify its perceptions. He listens for underlying meanings behind the spoken words and asks probing questions, leading the group to discover core obstacles and possible solutions. He challenges assumptions that block appropriate action. He connects teams with others who have conquered similar obstacles. Finally, the director employs problem solving skills and he passes on these skills to the team. He helps teams to turn obstacles into opportunities for change.

Practical Tools

The director can use the following practical tools to assist him in helping teams overcome obstacles:

1. Obstacle Reflection Wheel
2. Concrete vs. Illusory Venn Diagram
3. Obstacles Analysis and Solution Matrix
4. Creative Thinking Exercise
5. Obstacle Learnings Conversation

Practical Tool 1
Obstacle Reflection Wheel

Description

The director pulls out this tool when a group is facing one major obstacle. The wheel offers a guide for the number of sources of information that are needed for a group to come up with an adequate response to the obstacle. Once the wheel is completed, it is still necessary to make the leap to some form of appropriate actions and responses.

Example

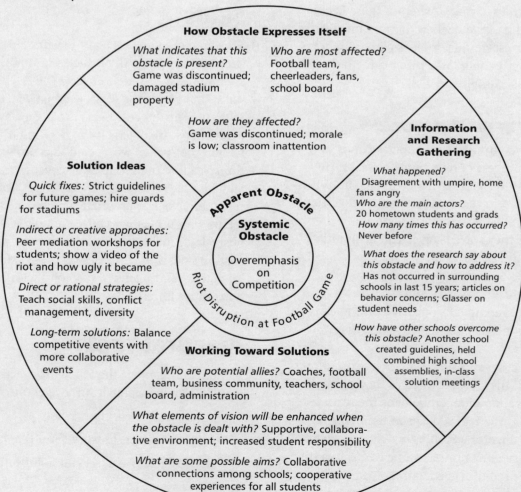

Instructions

Note: A blackline master of the Obstacle Reflection Wheel is provided in Appendix A, page 196.

1. Display an Obstacle Reflection Wheel.

2. Ask the group to name the apparent obstacle and write it on the wheel.

3. Challenge the group to name all of the ways this obstacle presents itself, using the questions on the wheel. Write answers on the wheel.

4. Guide the group to decide what the systemic obstacle is. Write this obstacle in the inner circle.

5. Ask the group questions under Information and Research Gathering. Write responses on the wheel.

6. Lead the group to begin working toward solutions using the questions on the wheel. Be sure to encourage the group to name positive aims rather than negative solutions (e.g., "establishing a peer mediation program" rather than "eliminating peer conflict"). Write responses on the wheel.

7. Encourage the group to amass solution ideas in four categories: quick fixes, indirect or creative approaches, direct or rational strategies, and long-term solutions. Write ideas on the wheel.

8. Lead the group to consensus on which solutions will be implemented. (If the group is having difficulty reaching a consensus, refer to *More Than 50 Ways to Build Team Consensus* by R. Bruce Williams [1993, pp. 107–108].) Write solutions on the wheel.

9. Process this tool with the group by asking the following questions:

   a. Which steps were most helpful to you?

   b. Which steps seemed to spark the most interest from the group?

   c. Where did the group struggle working on this process?

   d. What learnings have become clear about the process of addressing obstacles?

   e. What might we do differently next time?

Possible Uses

This tool can be used to tackle systemwide obstacles as well as irritants that are preventing team effectiveness. This tool can boost morale, because it helps the group focus on solutions. The tool can release the group to come up with creative solutions.

Practical Tool 2
Concrete vs. Illusory Venn Diagram

Description

The director uses this tool to distinguish between illusory and concrete obstacles. It is profitable to spend time distinguishing between concrete and illusory obstacles, so that the team does not waste time and energy chasing illusory obstacles.

Example

Concrete Obstacle   **Illusory Obstacle**

Obstacle and its resolution affects significant percentage of school community

Data can be compiled, making obstacle real

Resolution often involves fundamental shifts in the way education has been going on

Research backs up both the obstacle and the resolution strategies

Solution moves the school into the future

Generates concern and passion

Arises from a desire to improve education

Seems to paralyze change process

Feels overwhelming

Solutions never solve it; more obstacles keep appearing

Solution is often a return to the status quo or to the past

Obstacle and resolution impact only a few

Descriptions move from fear to fear

What is the obstacle?	What data supports the presence of the obstacle?	How many people are affected by the presence or removal of the obstacle?	What educational issues are involved?
What fears are supported by hard data?	What is the underlying aim of those voicing this concern?	What future direction or aim is causing this concern?	How willing are the constituencies to compromise?

Instructions

Note: A blackline master of the Concrete vs. Illusory Venn Diagram is provided in Appendix A, page 197.

1. Ask the group to choose an obstacle it is facing.

2. Lead the group through these questions:

   a. What is the obstacle?

   b. What data supports the presence of the obstacle?

   c. How many people are affected by the presence or removal of the obstacle?

   d. What educational issues are involved?

   e. What fears are supported by hard data?

   f. What is the underlying aim of those voicing this concern?

   g. What future direction or aim is causing this concern?

   h. How willing are the constituencies to compromise?

3. Direct the group to determine if the obstacle is illusory or concrete, using the answers to the above questions and the statements on the example Venn diagram.

4. Follow up as necessary. If the obstacle is illusory, some of the following questions might be useful:

   a. Who is most concerned and vocal about this obstacle?

   b. What are we hearing as their real concern?

   c. What are some principles or concerns in this area that seem reasonable and sound?

   d. How can we support at least some of these principles and concerns to reduce their fears?

   e. How can our actions include these principles and concerns?

Possible Uses

When a community voices concerns or presents obstacles, the director uses this tool to help teams determine whether obstacles are concrete or illusory. This helps the team to address and solve illusory obstacles early, instead of wasting time addressing phantom concerns.

Practical Tool 3
Obstacles Analysis and Solution Matrix

Description

The director and his team can use this tool to analyze major obstacles and to discern interrelationships among the obstacles. This allows the team to devise overall strategies to overcome many obstacles with just a few approaches. A few focused actions can have a greater impact than a myriad of unfocused actions.

Example

		Obstacle 1	Obstacle 2	Obstacle 3	Cross-Obstacle Reflection
Analysis	**Name**	Declining State Financial Support	Increasing Discipline Problems	Low Staff Morale	#1 and #2 Are Real Contributors to #3
	Symptoms	Budgets cut 10% after school sports dropped and class sizes increased 10%	Discipline referrals up 15%, chaotic halls, teachers estimate huge loss of instruction time	Difficulties in classroom management, declining attention spans, low parent support	Teachers obviously feeling overwhelmed and no sense of control
	Structural/ Systemic Block	Dependence on single source of revenue	Unengaged students whose only interests are outside of school	Pervasive sense of powerlessness	Many teachers and students are not engaged in learning
Solutions	**Potential Allies**	School board, administrators, teachers, community	Parents, teachers, community, administrators, students	Parents, community, teachers, students, administrators	Mobilizing the teachers and community is bottom line; increasing their sense of control is crucial
	Structural/ Systemic Solutions	Multisource revenue plan	Classes that engage students with varied instructional strategies	Site-based management or shared decision-making teams	Total staff participation along with community is crucial
	Resources Needed	Staff training, grant writing, community resources	Staff training and materials in varied instructional strategies, time for planning and support	Staff planning in shared decision-making, team meeting time	Staff training is central
	Next Steps	Multisource brainstorming workshop, community input	Team meeting to plan next year's training	Team meeting to plan next year's training	Participation by teams is key

Obstacles Analysis and Solution Matrix

Instructions

Note: A blackline master of the Obstacles Analysis and Solution Matrix is provided in Appendix A, page 198.

1. Display the Obstacles Analysis and Solution Matrix and give copies of the matrix to each individual or team. Ask the group to determine the major obstacles to include in the matrix. List them across the top row.

2. Assign one obstacle to each individual or team. Allow them fifteen minutes to complete their column on the matrix.

3. Ask individuals or teams to report on their obstacles. Fill in the displayed matrix.

4. Challenge the group to pick out similarities or connections between the columns. Note these reflections in the final column of the matrix.

5. Ask the group the following questions:

   a. What insights has this exercise revealed about overall approaches and strategies in dealing with these obstacles?

   b. What possible systemic solutions have been uncovered?

   c. What resources do we need?

   d. What action can we take to remove these obstacles?

6. Process this activity by asking: How has the use of this tool altered our thinking?

Possible Uses

This tool is particularly useful when teams have begun to implement changes, but have become overwhelmed by a number of obstacles. It is also appropriate for teams who are having difficulty seeing the big picture or discerning interrelationships between obstacles. This tool could be very influential to the action planning step if used in conjunction with a blocks brainstorming workshop and the naming of major blocks. This tool could then help determine what major directions the action planning could take.

Practical Tool 4
Creative Thinking Exercise

Description

The director pulls out this tool when a group has exhausted all of its possibilites and feels it has no other resources to conquer an obstacle. This tool arouses the group's creativity and enlarges thinking, leading them to discover potential solutions. (This tool is adapted from a method developed for use in training and facilitation, by Dorcas Rose, Eastern Regional Coordinator, Institute of Cultural Affairs.)

Example

Creative Thinking Exercise

Problem: How to win over five teachers who seem very closed to learning and using new instructional approaches.

Objects: A small abstract art piece and some music.

What do you see or hear? The art piece is red, brown, blue, and green. It looks like a lot of triangles hanging together. The music has a swinging movement. There are times that the music conveys humor.

What are the characteristics of the art piece and the music? The art piece is ordered, colorful, and bright. The music is smooth, inviting, lively, and fun.

How do the art piece and the music help us understand the obstacle? How are they like the problem? The rectangles in the art piece remind me of how traditional many of our teachers are. The lively, fun music reminds me that our students find our classes exactly the opposite.

How do the art object and piece of music give us clues to solutions? The teachers who are having a problem changing like the "order" in what they have been doing. Whatever we present to the faculty has to have a clear structure and order. We need to show that the teaching strategies we want to use are not only fun and inviting but also genuinely and positively impact student learning. We need to show students are learning while they are having fun in the classroom.

Solutions to the obstacle:

Team A	Team B	Team C
Begin to relate to the 5 teachers by asking for their advice	Initiate a peer coaching program	Make a video of a lively lesson
Invite the 5 teachers to visit other classrooms where new strategies are being used	Send these 5 teachers along with others to visit other schools	Spend 15 minutes sharing successes in each faculty meeting

Final Solutions: Make a video of lively lessons and begin to relate to the 5 teachers by asking for their advice.

Instructions

1. Set an art object or a toy out in the middle of the table.
   OR Play a piece of music.
   OR Have someone open the dictionary at random and point to a word.

2. Lead the group through this series of questions:

   a. Ask the group what they see or hear. (If it is a word, ask for other word associations.)

   b. What are the characteristics of this art object, toy, piece of music, or word?

   c. How does this art object, toy, piece of music, or word help us understand the obstacle? How is it like the problem?

   d. How does this art object, toy, piece of music, or word give us clues to solutions?

3. Record all responses on chart paper in front of the room. (If the group gets stuck on one item, choose a different one.)

4. Divide the group into teams. Direct teams to use the data generated from the questions to formulate two or three solutions to the obstacle.

5. Ask teams to share their solutions. The group may choose one or more solutions to implement.

6. Close with some processing questions:

   a. What happened during this activity?

   b. What did you like or dislike about this way of solving an obstacle?

   c. What was easy or hard about this methold?

   d. What did this activity do to our thinking?

   e. How might we use this again?

Possible Uses

Use this tool at the beginning of a meeting, when energy is high. This activity works well with groups that have a flexible mindset and are willing to try something different. This activity can be used to work on small irritants that seem to use up as much energy as the major obstacles.

Practical Tool 5
Obstacle Learnings Conversation

Description

This tool offers an opportunity for a group to process the experience they are having in implementation. This tool is a fine substitute for the Implementation Learnings Chart (chapter 6, tool 4). This conversation enables a group to see that it is growing in its ability to overcome obstacles.

Example

Obstacle Learnings Conversation

1. What obstacles have we been focusing on in these last months?

   a. Parents reluctance or inability to visit the school

   b. Board initially refused to support block scheduling

2. What actions and strategies have we been using?

   a. Career night (to involve parents and community members)
Student-led conferences

   b. Faculty report of visits to other schools doing block scheduling
Faculty summary report of research on block scheduling
Parent focus groups on block scheduling

3. What results have we been getting?

   a. 10% increase in parent attendance at Career Night
20% increase in average parent attendance at student led conferences

   b. Board is openly talking with us, but is not ready to approve
Many parents are asking us questions about block scheduling

4. What's been working?

   a. Events seem to spark parent attendance more than scheduled meetings

   b. Parent focus groups are generating much dialogue

5. Where have we been running into struggles or difficulties?

   a. Unclear how to reach parents in families where both parents work
Difficult for many single parents to get to the school

   b. Board is still struggling over the issue of block scheduling

---

(Continued on next page)

---

6. What have you been most pleased about in our efforts?

a. Career Night and student led conferences received enthusiastic responses from students, parents, and teachers
Career Night had wonderful support from the business community

b. Presentation by the faculty to the board was informative and fun

7. What have you been learning about challenging obstacles?

a. A thought-through plan is crucial
Often an action planned to impact one obstacle also affects other obstacles

b. Obstacles need to be challenged from many directions

8. What are some implications for our next few months?

a. Need to consult with some working parents about what strategies would help them connect more with the school

b. Need to meet with board members one to one and hear their real questions

---

Instructions

Ask the following questions, allowing several people to answer each one. As the questions progress, allow fifteen or twenty seconds for people to start answering each new question.

1. What obstacles have we been focusing on in these last months?

2. What actions and strategies have we been using?

3. What results have we been getting?

4. What's been working?

5. Where have we been running into struggles or difficulties?

6. What have you been most pleased about in our efforts?

7. What have you been learning about challenging obstacles?

8. What are some implications for our next few months?

Possible Uses

If a group has had a particularly difficult job implementing its action plan, this conversation could reveal to the group how much they have accomplished as well as how much they have learned. This conversation could be held right after a series of team reports on the last implementation time period. It could also occur just before some new planning is to take place. The underlying intent is to help the group to realize how many resources reside right in the group itself.

Case Study

Striking a Blow to Apathy

Teachers in a suburban community had been working all year to implement an alternative assessment model. They had students add work to their portfolios all year long. To showcase the students' work, the teachers planned a Portfolio Night in early May.

The teachers wanted to improve dialogue between parents and students, because parents did not understand the real content of what students were studying. The teachers also hoped to encourage more parents to attend, because only 60–70 percent of the parents usually attended school events.

When the director showed up a month before the event, little serious planning had taken place. His first step was to show the teachers a video that featured a school that had held student-led conferences. The teachers were inspired by the video and began to form concrete and detailed plans for the Portfolio Night.

The planners advertised the Portfolio Night in the PTA newsletter and a flyer. Students made and delivered invitations to their parents. Teachers guided students to choose the best items for their portfolios. They also helped students create presentation plans and allowed them to role play what they would do and say.

When parents arrived at the Portfolio Night, they were given a program flyer that included instructions on how to encourage their child's presentations and how to ask pertinent questions. As students presented their work, the teachers acted only as facilitators. The students were the stars for the night. To wrap up the evening, the PTA sponsored an ice cream social to honor the students' accomplishments.

The Portfolio Night was an overwhelming success—99 percent of the students had at least one adult show up that night. Parents were intrigued with and proud of all their children were learning and accomplishing. Parents who had not come to the school in years came to this Portfolio Night.

The teachers successfully overcame their targeted obstacles—improving dialogue between students and parents about schoolwork and boosting attendance at school events. They also unwittingly improved teacher morale and deepened their motivation. A veteran teacher with twenty-five years experience explained that the Portfolio Night was one of the five highlights of her career. Without knowing it, the teachers and students created an event which told the whole community that exciting things were going on in that school.

Chapter 9

The Promoter Advertises Successes

The Promoter is the Resource Consultant who focuses on communicating visible achievements.

Role Description

The promoter encourages educators to share what is happening, how it is happening, what is working, and what is not. The promoter assists schools in connecting with one another, so that they may help each other in their restructuring journeys. The promoter also encourages community organizations to get connected to the school.

Eliminating Isolation and Building Alliances

Educators have been demoralized by the isolation they experience in the educational system (Fullan 1991). Teachers and schools create some ingenious strategies, but competition, mistrust, and top-down bureaucracy often prevent them from sharing their ideas. They do not know what is happening in other schools or districts, because schools and districts fail to communicate with each other. And few educators break out of their isolation by subscribing to professional publications or attending regional or national conferences.

The promoter seeks to lift educators out of their isolation by connecting teachers with teachers, schools with schools, and districts with districts. She encourages teachers to share ideas and to adapt successful strategies from each other. As teachers learn of others' successes and struggles, they gain confidence. The promoter builds networks of schools and districts so that teachers, principals, and administrators can exchange problem-solving, technical, or financial strategies. When schools and districts connect with one another, perspectives are challenged, dialogue is fostered, and new successes are generated.

The promoter realizes that "seeing is believing." She encourages educators to visit other schools to see change in action. Many teachers have created ingenious strategies, but often these strategies remain hidden by competition and mistrust. The promoter connects schools with other schools that have worked through similar problems. Exchanging stories, accomplishments, and learnings not only gives educators new ideas but also encourages them to take risks.

Connecting Schools with Outside Sources

The promoter not only promotes alliances among educators, but she also creates mutually beneficial connections with every sector of the community. Schools cannot function apart from business and community support; alliances between schools and other sectors are crucial.

All successful change processes are characterized by collaboration and close interaction among those central to carrying out the changes. If we are to accomplish change in education we have to, in Bruce Joyce's coruscating phrase, 'crack the walls of privatism.' Privatism and professional development are closely and inversely linked. Alliances provide greater power, both of ideas and of the ability to act on them.

. . . some of the most powerful strategies involve inter-institutional partnerships—between school districts and universities, businesses and districts, coalitions of schools, and so on. (Fullan 1991, p. 349)

We no longer live in a compartmentalized society. To survive, all sectors of the community must connect, network, and work together. Businesses depend on schools to provide skilled workers. Schools depend on communities to provide financial support. Communities depend on schools to draw people into the area. Schools and communities depend on businesses to provide employment and a viable economy. The school cannot be successful without the full involvement of the community (Byham 1992). "There is no question that the problems of reform are insurmountable without a dramatic increase in the number of alliances practicing positive politics" (Fullan 1991, p. 350).

The promoter builds alliances among schools, businesses, and communities. She encourages educators to come out from their isolation and create new networks. The greater the alliances, the greater the chance of creating imaginative solutions with broader collaborative support (Morgan 1986). As teachers connect with communities and businesses, attitudes change. Business people and community members begin to see how dedicated and professional teachers are, and teachers begin to realize that business people and community members are deeply concerned about the future of students.

Modeling Collaboration

The promoter demonstrates collaboration. Schools that have been models of individualism and competition need demonstrations of what collaboration looks and feels like. The promoter models the very sharing and collaboration she is attempting to foster: she demonstrates techniques for sharing; she praises and advertises collaborative efforts between teachers, businesses, and communities; she uses collaborative language, promoting "our" successes rather than "my" successes and "our" challenges rather than "your" challenges.

The promoter remains optimistic and models collaboration when others cling to individualism. She respects teachers' hesitancy to share successful lessons. She knows that some may protest by saying, "Why should I tell other teachers about something I worked hours on to prepare for my students? Let them figure something out on their own!" Instead of forcing teachers to work together, the promoter gently points out that sharing information can lighten the teacher's load. The teacher's job can become easier when teachers, businesses, the community, and other schools share wisdom and work together.

Sustaining Lifelines of Communication

Effective communication builds and sustains alliances.

Communicate, communicate, communicate. Schooling involves everyone in the community. Inundate everyone in the community with information. Those who are expert will find the information useful (they can at least sort through it). Those who are not will be either flattered or bored, and in any case they will leave you alone. (Doyle and Pimentel 1993, p. 539)

The producer invests time and effort in keeping in touch with every sector of the school and the community, including teachers, staff, students, administration, business partners, and volunteers.

The promoter creates comprehensible and usable communications. She condenses long reports into useful charts or graphs. She writes timely and focused informational pieces. Her communication is genuinely helpful and informative, and readers look forward to hearing from her.

The promoter also helps educators become effective communicators. She guides schools to write their own stories that report their successes and failures. She encourages schools to create restructuring portfolios comprising authentic artifacts that demonstrate steps on the journey and victories along the way.

When This Role Is Needed

The promoter steps in to help when a school needs to see how another school or district implemented change. The promoter can also help a school change team that is discouraged by an overwhelming obstacle. Connecting this team with other schools or districts can dramatize how far the team has come and how it might work to overcome the obstacle. This role is also crucial when two or more schools are heading in a similar direction and are interested in sharing resources. The promoter uses this role when the school needs to pull its victory story together so that others can join in the support of the school.

Skills

The promoter's primary skill is creatively connecting schools with the community. She firmly believes that isolated schools cannot survive. She discerns what needs of the school the community, businesses, or other school organizations can fulfill. The promoter is also an excellent communicator and she teaches these skills to those who work with her.

Practical Tools

The promoter can use the following practical tools to assist her in advertising successes and connecting teams with resources:

1. Network Source Triangle
2. Network Visual
3. Network Benefits Chart
4. Reporting Format for School-to-School Sharing
5. Debriefing a Network on School Participation

Practical Tool 1
Network Source Triangle

Description

The promoter uses this tool to get the group thinking about potential networks in the community. This tool helps educators realize that they are already connected to many resources that are available within and outside of the school. (The three categories are adapted from "Facilitating Social Change" by D. Holmes [1996, pp. 2–4] and *Winning Through Participation* by L. J. Spencer [1989, p. 128].)

Example

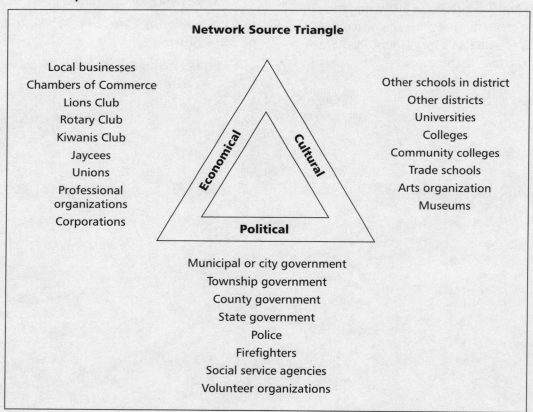

Network Source Triangle

Local businesses
Chambers of Commerce
Lions Club
Rotary Club
Kiwanis Club
Jaycees
Unions
Professional organizations
Corporations

Other schools in district
Other districts
Universities
Colleges
Community colleges
Trade schools
Arts organization
Museums

Economical

Cultural

Political

Municipal or city government
Township government
County government
State government
Police
Firefighters
Social service agencies
Volunteer organizations

Instructions

1. Draw a triangle on a piece of chart paper. Label the left side Economical, the right side Cultural, and the bottom Political.

2. Ask the group to brainstorm seven to ten potential networks in each category.

3. Divide the group into teams of four or five. Direct teams to place stars beside the networks they have personal connections to. Ask teams to pick the two connections from each section that they have the best connections to.

4. Ask the group to choose the three best networks from each section.

5. Assign teams of two or three to work on each network. Teams can meet for twenty minutes to decide what steps to take to connect with that network. (They might work together on the Network Benefits Chart [see tool 3] to discern what mutual benefits such a connection could offer.)

6. Process this workshop with some of the following questions:

   a. What did we accomplish?

   b. What pleased or excited you?

   c. What surprised you?

   d. What did we learn from this workshop?

   e. How will we be different as we make some of these network connections?

Possible Uses

The promoter uses this activity at the beginning of a new venture, especially when the school is feeling isolated and unsupported. Getting connected with other schools and with networks in the community can offer support, information, and human resources needed to move into this new phase. The promoter may also employ this tool when a team wants to publicize a victory, a phase, or a program segment. The team can also brainstorm possible networks that should receive publicity.

Practical Tool 2
Network Visual

Description

This tool helps teams visualize present and future connections to other schools, businesses, and community organizations. Creating this visual can make the potential of network connections more real to the team.

Example

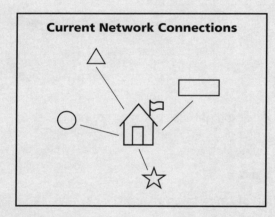

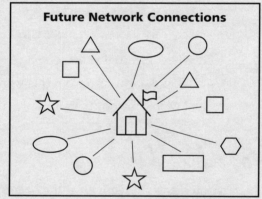

Instructions

1. Draw a representation of the school in the center of a large piece of chart paper. Title the drawing Current Network Connections.

2. Ask the group to brainstorm networks that currently support the school. Create different shapes to represent different networks or different kinds of networks (e.g., squares for other schools, triangles for the business community, circles for organizations, stars for arts groups, etc.). Write the networks on the shapes and tape them to the chart paper.

3. Use yarn to connect the shapes with the school. Use a different color of yarn to designate the kind of connection the network offers. For example, blue might represent adults visiting the classroom, green might represent students spending time in the community, red might represent staff members participating in training, and orange might represent sharing ideas between schools.

4. Create a second visual to represent the connections the school would like to make in the next year. Ask the group to brainstorm networks that the school intends to build and encourage in the coming year and the kinds of connections those networks would offer. Label the drawing Future Network Connections.

5. Display the visuals side by side. Process the meeting with the following questions:

   a. What do you notice about the two visuals?

   b. What surprises you or intrigues you about the visuals?

   c. What do these visuals reveal to us?

   d. How have these visuals challenged your thinking about networks?

   e. What are the implications for us as a school?

Possible Uses

The promoter uses this tool when teams need encouragement to be more connected to outside resources. The tool is especially pertinent when a school experiences a loss of financial support or is facing overwhelming demands. This tool can demonstrate to educators that schools do not have to go it alone; potential support and information surrounds the school.

Practical Tool 3
Network Benefits Chart

Description

This brainstorming tool demonstrates to educators that networks and schools benefit when alliances are formed. The promoter can use this tool to help educators see how they may help the community and how the community may help them.

Example

Network Benefits Chart		
Specific Network	**Benefit(s) to Network**	**Benefit(s) to School**
Local businesses	Source of future employees; employee networking	Apprenticeship training for students; mentoring
Senior citizens	Significant use of time	Assistance in classrooms (reading, math, etc.)
Universities and colleges	Practice teaching opportunities; further training	Staff development and training
Kiwanis, Jaycees, Rotary, Lions	Program speakers	Specific project support
Police	Positively connects young people and police	Drug/law enforcement programs

Instructions

Note: A blackline master of the Network Benefits Chart is provided in Appendix A, page 199.

1. Ask the group to name some possible networks. List these on chart paper in front of the room.

2. Divide the group into teams. Assign one or two networks to each of the teams. Allow teams time to brainstorm how the network and the school might benefit from each of their assigned networks.

3. Ask teams to share their lists. Post all the information on a chart so that all teams may see it. Invite additional insights from the group.

4. Process the information by proposing the following questions:

   a. What was easy about coming up with benefits? What was hard?

   b. What benefits surprise you or intrigue you?

   c. What insights did you gain from compiling this benefit list?

   d. How has this activity changed your thinking about networks?

   e. Why have we focused so much attention on articulating network benefits?

Possible Uses

The promoter pulls out this tool when teachers still desire to remain isolated. She uses the tool to dramatize the advantages of creative connections—advantages for the student, the teacher, and the community. She can also employ this tool to get educators excited about making new connections. Naming benefits allows educators to "show off" what they can offer the community.

Practical Tool 4
Reporting Format
for School-to-School Sharing

Description

This tool offers a guideline for how schools can share accomplishments with other schools in a concise and powerful way. This format keeps the report focused, upbeat, and informative. This format can be the basis of ongoing written communications or can be adapted for face-to-face meetings with groups of teachers from different schools.

Example

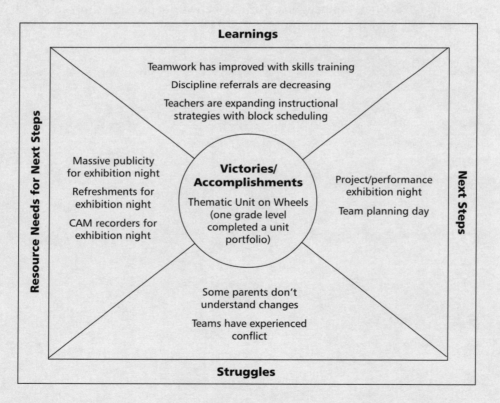

Learnings

Teamwork has improved with skills training

Discipline referrals are decreasing

Teachers are expanding instructional strategies with block scheduling

Resource Needs for Next Steps

Massive publicity for exhibition night

Refreshments for exhibition night

CAM recorders for exhibition night

Victories/ Accomplishments

Thematic Unit on Wheels (one grade level completed a unit portfolio)

Next Steps

Project/performance exhibition night

Team planning day

Some parents don't understand changes

Teams have experienced conflict

Struggles

Instructions

Note: A blackline master of the Reporting Format for School-to-School Sharing is provided in Appendix A, page 200.

1. Distribute a blank school-to-school reporting format to each team. Ask teams to fill out the formats. (You may choose to have teams draw large formats on chart paper, so that they may display their work to the other teams.) Teams may choose to add visuals to the verbal report for extra emphasis.

2. Direct teams to share their reports with the group.

3. After four or five reports are given, stop the reporting and ask some of these processing questions:

   a. Which things that you heard particularly stuck in your mind?

   b. Which of these things interest or intrigue you?

   c. What are the reports saying about what's happening with our students, our teachers, or our teacher teams?

   d. What questions are starting to emerge for you?

4. Finally, when all the reports are shared, allow ten or fifteen minutes for teachers to seek out other teachers to hear more about a particular report.

5. At the conclusion, you might ask one or two final processing questions.

   a. What was valuable to you from today's reporting time?

   b. What is all this saying about what is happening in the field of education today?

Possible Uses

School-to-school sharing is becoming as crucial today as teacher-to-teacher sharing and interaction. Not only is it important for an elementary school to share with other elementary schools, but elementary schools also need to share with middle and high schools, high schools with elementary and middle schools, and middle with elementary and high schools. Districts may choose to spend the first hour of its district staff meetings doing this kind of reporting and sharing.

Practical Tool 5
Debriefing a Network on School Participation

Description

The promoter uses this tool to debrief a network at the midpoint of a project or when the project is completed. This tool reveals how the network and the school benefited from the project.

Example

Debriefing a Network on School Participation	
Network: Local Bank	
1. What are some reports you heard from your employees?	• When they visited classrooms, they were surprised at the number and depth of the questions that the students asked. • The students who worked here were all conscientious and dependable.
2. What did they like? What pleased them?	• They appreciated connections with teenagers. • They enjoyed the opportunities to show students how their school skills will help them in the workplace.
3. What struggles did they enounter?	• A few students refused to pay attention. • They were shocked at the poor physical condition of some of our school facilities.
4. How do your colleagues talk about how they have helped our school?	• They believe they are making learning more relevant. • They believe they are teaching many aspects of the work ethic.
5. How has this connection with our schools been a benefit for you?	• The employees return to the bank very motivated and upbeat. They seem to work twice as hard. • We're meeting young people we want to hire in the future.
6. How could we improve this program next year?	• Keep the same employee connected to the same class for at least a semester. • We would like to participate with you in interviewing students interested in part-time work with us.

Instructions

Note: A blackline master of Defriefing a Network on School Participation is provided in Appendix A, page 201.

1. Use the form to help teachers and administrators debrief network representatives after network projects are completed. In other words, this form can guide a conversation involving a teacher, an adminstrator, and a network representative.

2. Keep these forms as an ongoing record of how network connections are progressing.

3. Ask a team to review the forms periodically. Teams should look for common themes and for clues on how to improve network connections.

4. Use the information gained from the debriefing to write articles or promotional pieces about the school. (Be sure to get the network's permission before publicizing the information.) You could also articulate the benefits listed on the forms to new network possibilities.

Possible Uses

The promoter uses this form with established connections to make sure things are going smoothly. She may also use it every few months with new network connections to be sure that the connection is mutually beneficial. With the permission of the network, the information gathered can be used as a basis for an article or for a radio or television feature.

Case Study

Removing the Walls
Between the School and the Community

In the following examples, the enthusiastic promoter (facilitator) is the key to making connections. She inspires networks to want a connection with the schools, by tapping into their desires to provide great opportunities for children. She fashions genuine and reasonable requests that clarify how the network will benefit from the connection. She invites others to become a part of a winning strategy, because everyone desires to win.

The following alliances and connections have been made by promoters in recent years:

- People from the business community volunteering time to go into the classroom and help students with basic skills.

- Businesses offering apprenticeship programs. Students are given part-time jobs that may lead to full-time employment after graduation.

- Companies offering scholarship assistance for post-secondary education. These opportunites are tied to specific job offers after graduation.

- Senior citizens assisting elementary students in reading programs and also serving as "foster grandparents." In return for such assistance, the school may offer, for example, to open its hallways for senior citizens to use for walking.

- Companies assisting students in "invention fairs" enabling the students to create highly imaginative and educational models and machines.

- Schools offering parenting classes to help parents upgrade their skills.

- Schools holding a Career Night so that parents and community members can acquaint students with various occupations.

- Zoos bringing safe, live animals to classrooms to acquaint students with animal life.

Part 4

Group Energizer

Introduction

Many people experience work conditions devoid of energy and enthusiasm.

> 'The signs are everywhere; people are at the end of the line in what they're willing to give up in their humanity,' says Jeremy Rifkin, an economist and author of *The End of Work* . . . 'The mental fatigue today is every bit as significant as the physical fatigue of the early Industrial Revolution.'
>
> In some two dozen interviews for this story—mostly white-collar, Chicago professionals in their 30s and 40s—the overload was palpable. Respondents used medical terms to describe themselves ('brain dead,' 'hemorrhaging') and their workplaces ('triage,' 'trauma ward'). (Rubin 1995, p. 11)

Educators are also paralyzed by this inner malaise. "The message is clear: the problem isn't work, it's fulfillment" (Rubin 1995, p. 13). Educators often do not sense that what they are doing is meaningful and significant.

> Technological breakthroughs have created previously unknown conveniences and efficiencies. Yet we still face an onslaught of problems that are frustratingly resistant to rational and technical solutions. . . . More and more of us see that many of these problems are rooted in a disease of the human spirit. (Bolman and Deal 1995, p. 166)

The group energizer seeks to reconnect educators with meaning and significance in their work. He challenges educators to rediscover their original motivations for becoming teachers. He helps them understand that their most effective resources are found within their situation and within themselves. The task, the team, and the results can also be sources of energy for school change. When the group energizer continually brings spirit, purpose, and meaning to the surface, energy emerges to complete the tasks.

The road to school change is long and challenging. The twentieth century has wrought rapid and complex changes to the world, but schools have often resisted these changes. Bringing schools up to date requires years of work. Consequently, the group energizer's task is to keep educators motivated for their tasks for years to come.

The group energizer uses tools as simple as a surprise lunch or as complex as a weekend planning retreat to keep people believing and hoping in realistic possibilities. The group energizer stays alert to the fluctuating moods and recurring doubts of teams so that he might meet them with enouragement. He ensures that teams stay energized for the long haul.

> There must be encouragement, support in the form of new resources, the sharing of experiences, and drummers to sustain the march when energies flag. There is nothing mysterious about these ingredients. But it is probably futile to attempt educational improvement without them. (Goodlad 1994, p. 638)

In addition to these skills, the group energizer needs a powerful "will"—a desire to act (Miles and Louis 1990). Actions produce change and creative solutions to overwhelming problems. The group energizer convinces teams that efforts toward school change truly improve students' learning. He emphasizes over and again that changes are happening and victories are being won.

The group energizer is so important that he can make up for some of the gaps in the process leader, the skills trainer, and the resource consultant. If he is genuine and caring, he can encourage teams and can energize them for the continuing challenge of school change.

The group energizer may take on three roles—conductor, concertmaster, or critic. The conductor keeps teams focused on their original plans and purposes. The concertmaster works with teams to create a harmonious work environment. The critic celebrates the team's performance.

Chapter 10

The Conductor Stays True to the Score

The Conductor is the Group Energizer who focuses on student learning and achievement.

Role Description

The conductor ensures that school change initiators stay true to their original plans for school change. He reminds teams that the real purpose for school change is to enhance student learning and achievement. He advises them to assess situations, problems, and possibilities realistically. He questions if plans are doable and in accordance with objective data and research. When momentary setbacks threaten to overwhelm them, he motivates educators to consider the whole picture and to see the progress they have made. When school change advocates feel discouraged by long projects or become bogged down by mundane tasks, the conductor helps them see how far they've come.

Aprising the Real Situation

The conductor helps the school change team honestly assess their situation. He keeps teams from falling victim to grandiosity or despair.

Grandiosity leads a team to develop wild, overblown plans that have no basis in reality. The conductor redirects grandios planners to consider

objective data about the situation and to appraise the limitations and road blocks they may encounter. The conductor ensures that tasks, projects, and objectives remain faithful to the real situation. Even when the purpose is commendable, energy immediately disappears when tasks are unrealistic—nothing saps energy faster than unrealistic expectations.

Despair causes teams to lose hope and the ability to see beyond minor irritations. The conductor reveals signs of hope and growth amidst problems to encourage despairing teams. Even when the real situation is filled with bad news, honestly honoring the facts can create energy.

> I've seen leaders make great efforts to speak forthrightly and frequently to employees about current struggles, about the tough times that lie ahead, and about what they dream of for the future. These conversations fill a painful period with new purpose, giving reasons for the current need to sacrifice and hold on. In most cases, given this kind of meaningful information, workers respond with allegiance and energy. (Wheatley 1992, p. 135)

When teams feel that they know the truth about the situation, they willingly volunteer for tasks and projects that will make a difference. The conductor makes sure that the facts are shared openly, because he knows that honesty engenders trust and trust engenders energy for the tasks at hand.

Thwarting Attempts to Retreat

Teams may be tempted to retreat when implementation has begun and obstacles loom.

> A phase of initial embracing is followed by anxiety. The anxiety, when strong enough, causes individuals to retreat to the security of familiar ways of doing things, a kind of 'coming home.' But upon arriving home, there is a sense that things are not the same anymore. An unsettling feeling of dissatisfaction then causes an individual to venture out again to explore new assumptions and reframe existing ones. (Gallegos 1994, p. 35)

The conductor reminds the team that there is no going back. Perspectives have changed; eyes have been opened. A vision of something new is starting to grow. Things can never be the same again.

The temptation to retreat stems from the human desire for comfort and familiarity. Change feels unsettling. The conductor seeks to lessen the anxiety and the unfamiliarity that accompanies change. He leads teams to visualize themselves a few years into the future when they will be experiencing the accomplishments of their change efforts (Miles and Louis 1990). He knows team members can become more comfortable with change when they can imagine the results of the change. The conductor helps people imagine what the future will look and sound like.

Focusing on the Core Task

The conductor continually reminds teams that their fundamental purpose is to improve student learning and achievement. Teams in the midst of endless, time-consuming, and overwhelming tasks often forget why they began these tasks. Small obstacles look larger and recovery from setbacks takes longer. Teams begin to feel helpless. "Beneath [this] helplessness is a spiritual vacuum. It saps our faith, weakens our heart, and leaves us foundering" (Bolman and Deal 1995, p. 59).

The conductor understands that connecting teams with their core purpose reconnects them to the energy they need to overcome obstacles. He leads conversations and reflective exercises that help teams rediscover their original hopes, aspirations, and purposes. As teams reconnect with their inner purposes, they become energized to return to the tasks at hand.

The conductor also chooses appropriate moments to connect teams with the significance of their ongoing tasks.

> If we search to create meaning, we can survive and even flourish. In chaotic organizations, I observed just such a phenomenon. Employees were wise enough to sense that personal meaning-making was their only route out of chaos. (Wheatley 1992, pp. 134–135)

The conductor poses questions that lead the team to discover meaning in its tasks. He knows that while it may seem simpler for him to offer his own ideas, the team gains energy when it grapples to create its own meaning and significance.

> You can't impose significance. People have to create it together. . . . The responsibility of the guide is not to give answers, but to raise questions, suggest directions to explore, and to offer support. (Bolman and Deal, 1995 pp. 96, 170)

The conductor's overall goal is to humanize the change process so that educators are energized by their work. As he connects teams with their situations, their needs, and their sense of meaning, they experience fulfillment in their work. "Individuals and groups, like biological organisms, operate most effectively only when their needs are satisfied" (Morgan 1986, p. 41).

When This Role Is Needed

The conductor steps in when planning euphoria overtakes a team and it decides to schedule twenty projects when it can realistically handle three. The conductor also encourages the team that is hesitant to plan more than one project when it has the resources to do ten. He steps in when the team has lost sight of the big picture and has forgotten why it is pursuing change. He helps teams connect their original priorities with their real situation.

Skills

The conductor focuses the team on the real situation, the real challenges, and the real possibilities surrounding the task of increasing student learning and achievement. He skillfully applies tools and approaches that reveal potential limits and blocks as well as reasonable and attainable possibilities in the situation at hand. He asks questions that connect teams to their sources of energy and motivation. The conductor is known for his ability to reveal options in the worst of situations.

Practical Tools

The conductor can use the following practical tools to assist him in guiding teams to stay true to their original purposes and plans for school change:

1. Real Situation Chart
2. Why We Can't Go Back
3. Reasons Why Conversation
4. What Pulls You Through Conversation

Practical Tool 1
The Real Situation Chart

Description

This tool helps teams discover the limitations of their situation and develop plans that account for these limitations.

Example

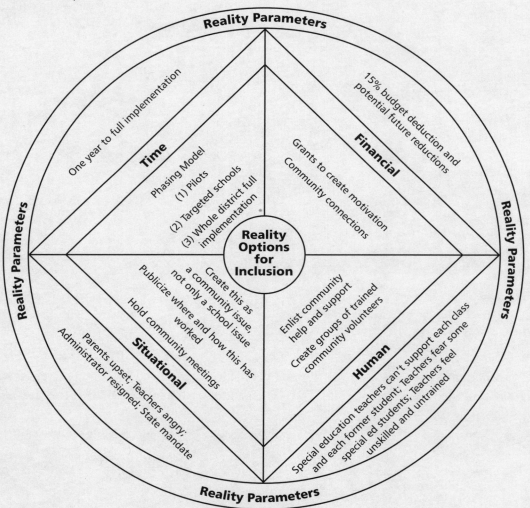

Instructions

Note: A blackline master of The Real Situation Chart is provided in Appendix A, page 202.

1. Display The Real Situation Chart for the group. Divide the group into four teams. Assign each team to brainstorm the parameters of one of the topics (time, money/materials, human, or situation).

2. Ask teams to share their brainstorming ideas. Write their ideas on the chart. Ask the group to share any additional ideas for each of the four categories.

3. Lead the group to process the information, using the following questions:

   a. Do you see an overall pattern or gain an overall perpsective from these parameters?

   b. Do the parameters give any clues for taking the next step?

4. Provide five minutes for individual brainstorming on possible reality options (e.g., possible ways to proceed within the parameters).

5. Direct individuals to share their ideas with their teams.

6. Ask teams to report their reality options to the whole group. Write these options on the chart.

7. Lead the group to choose options that seem to account for the parameters and provide workable options.

8. Process this activity by discussing these questions:

   a. How were we stuck before?

   b. What happened to us during this activity?

   c. How did it happen?

   d. How has your thinking been altered?

   e. When might we reuse this activity or a similar activity?

Possible Uses

The conductor uses this tool when a group is totally overwhelmed by or is completely ignorant of the limitations of a situation. When a group runs into a situation they feel is impossible, this tool can help them discover possible solutions.

Practical Tool 2
Why We Can't Go Back

Description

This tool energizes teams to remember why they chose to pursue change. In this activity, team members discuss new possibilites, remember the old situation, and rediscover their reasons for chosing a new path.

Example

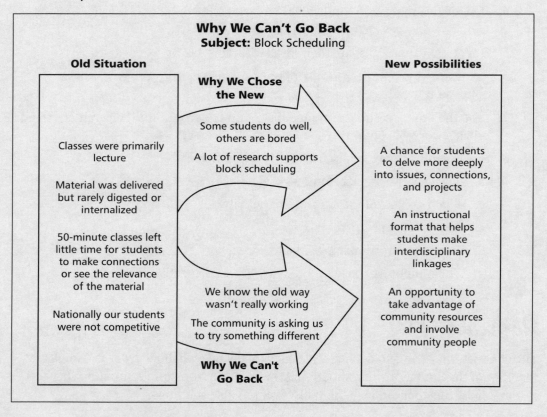

Why We Can't Go Back
Subject: Block Scheduling

Old Situation

New Possibilities

Why We Chose the New

Classes were primarily lecture

Material was delivered but rarely digested or internalized

50-minute classes left little time for students to make connections or see the relevance of the material

Nationally our students were not competitive

Some students do well, others are bored

A lot of research supports block scheduling

A chance for students to delve more deeply into issues, connections, and projects

An instructional format that helps students make interdisciplinary linkages

We know the old way wasn't really working

The community is asking us to try something different

An opportunity to take advantage of community resources and involve community people

Why We Can't Go Back

Instructions

Note: A blackline master of Why We Can't Go Back is provided in Appendix A, page 203.

1. Divide the group into teams of two or three. Direct teams to discuss the new possibilties offered by the implementation program(s) they began. (Begin discussing new possibilties rather than discussing the old situation; teams become more energized when they focus on positive future events.)

2. Ask teams to share their thinking with the whole group. Record their ideas under New Possibilities.

3. Follow up with one of these questions:

   a. What about these new possibilities were you reminded of during this conversation?

   b. What had you forgotten about during these last few weeks?

4. Allow time for teams to brainstorm elements and characteristics from the old situation. Ask teams to share their ideas with the whole group. Record responses in the Old Situation column.

5. Follow up with these questions:

   a. What did you discover about the old situation that you weren't aware of before?

   b. When you compare the new possibilites with the old situation, what do you notice that you never noticed before?

6. Ask the whole group to explain why they chose the new. Write responses on the upper arrow.

7. Ask the group to explain why they can't go back. Write responses on the lower arrow.

8. Process the activity with the following questions:

   a. What surprised you about this activity and conversation?

   b. What did you discover about how your thinking has shifted?

   c. What have you learned?

   d. What are we saying about why we can't go back?

   e. Why do you feel *you* can't go back?

Possible Uses

This tool is a great energizer for teams that are facing obstacles and that need encouragement to keep working for change. If the change process has been especially grueling, the group may decide to record the results of this activity on a poster. This visual reminder can add energy to a group in the midst of challenging circumstances. People need reminders of why they chose to pursue new possibilities and why they cannot retreat once they begin to change.

Practical Tool 3
Reasons Why Conversation

Description

This tool leads educators to rediscover their original motivations and aspirations for their career. As educators share their dreams with one another, they become motivated to pursue their goals.

Example

Reasons Why Conversation

1. **How long have you been teaching (or in education)?**
   12 years + 1 year + 35 years + 26 years + 15 years = 89 years!

2. **List some of the high points in your career.**
   - The year I taught science to an at-risk class
   - The role I had as department head
   - When I taught a third grade class one year and had the same class for fourth grade the next year
   - The year I team taught with a good friend

3. **List some of the low points in your career.**
   - The year I couldn't get anywhere with a particular student
   - Three years with a principal who wouldn't listen to the teachers
   - My first year trying to introduce new teaching strategies to my classes
   - The year I struggled with four sets of angry parents

4. **Describe what things have helped you stay in education.**
   - I've liked working with the age group of children I have.
   - I know that when I work with children, I am helping to influence the future.
   - Working with my colleagues has helped me stay.
   - The communication I get with students after they graduate thrills me.

5. **What inspired you to become an educator?**
   - My seventh grade teacher influenced me.
   - My home life was not happy, but school made up for it.
   - I felt how much a teacher can help a child grow.

6. **What has helped you to become open to the new decisions we have been making and the new directions we are going in?**
   - I have seen many students succeed, but I've always been concerned about those who don't.
   - I've tried some new things in my class, and they have made a positive difference.
   - I'm worried that our students are not comparing very well with many students from other countries.

7. **What beliefs about teaching and education do you adhere to today?**
   - Many educators are saying this, but I truly believe "all children can learn."
   - I believe that we need to teach basics, but we also need to teach much more.
   - Education needs to be compatible with the current research on the brain.
   - Education needs to be dynamic and challenge everyone's thinking. It needs to stress skills and processes, not just facts.

(Continued on next page)

8. **Processing questions:**
   a. **How was the group affected by this discussion?**
      • Our mood became more serious.
      • We were proud of our colleagues' high points.
      • We really connected with some of the things our colleagues said.

   b. **What shifted in us during this conversation?**
      • We hardly get a chance to talk like this during the busy days we have at school. This conversation brought us closer together as a team.
      • I felt like I got to know people better than I ever have.
      • We began to appreciate the gifts our colleagues bring to teaching.

   c. **What happened to our energy level as we discussed these questions?**
      • We began with very animated responses.
      • We were quiet and sober when we talked about low points.
      • There was a quiet excitement as we shared our beliefs about teaching and education.

Instructions

1. Lead the group through each of the following questions. Solicit several responses for each question. (The earlier questions are easier and may generate more responses than the later questions.)

   a. How long have you been teaching (or in education)? (You may choose to add up the years of experience so that the group can get a picture of the total number of years represented in the group.)

   b. List some of the high points in your career.

   c. List some of the low points in your career.

   d. Describe what things have helped you stay in education?

   e. What inspired you to become an educator?

   f. What has helped you to become open to the new decisions we have been making and the new directions we are going in?

   g. What beliefs about teaching and education do you adhere to today?

2. Process the discussion with one or two of the following questions:

   a. How was the group affected by this discussion?

   b. What shifted in us during this conversation?

   c. What happened to our energy level as we discussed these questions?

Possible Uses

This tool can generate energy and excitement for groups that have been working together for awhile; however, team members must trust one another and be willing to share with one another for this tool to be effective. The conductor may employ this tool to celebrate the completion of a major task or to honor a team member who made a significant step in his career. He may also choose this tool when team members need to gain perspective after a major setback.

Practical Tool 4
What Pulls You Through Conversation

Description

The What Pulls You Through Conversation leads educators through a series of questions aimed at revealing their reasons for staying in education. As group members share with one another, they discover how others keep themselves motivated and they begin to see why they should continue the school change journey.

Example

What Pulls You Through Questionnaire

1. **What tasks take up a lot of your time?**
   - Lesson planning
   - Office paperwork
   - Discipline issues
   - Grading papers

2. **Which of these tasks are a worthwhile use of your time? What would you like to spend your time doing?**
   - I like spending time teaching students.
   - I enjoy putting a unit together.
   - I always appreciate one-to-one conversations with students.
   - It is stimulating to work on a project with my colleagues.

3. **Which of these tasks are not a worthwhile use of your time? What would you rather *not* spend time doing?**
   - I always begrudge the paperwork, because I think of what else I could be doing with my time.
   - Some meetings seem to be a waste of time.
   - I wish there was a good way to grade papers that didn't take so much time.

4. **In what moments are you most discouraged? At what points are you ready to give up?**
   - I get discouraged when students don't seem to be making any progress.
   - It's disappointing when the standardized test scores go down.
   - I always get upset when students with great promise drop out of school.

5. **What do you tell yourself that helps you continue? What do you do for yourself that helps you go on?**
   - I remind myself that I'm doing this for the sake of the students.
   - I remind myself of teachers who made such an impact on me.
   - I think about the home life many of these students have and realize we may be the best thing going for them.

(Continued on next page)

6. **Processing questions:**

   a. **How was the group affected by this discussion?**
   - We had an easier time talking about what we don't like.
   - We got very lively talking about both the things we like to do and the things we don't like to do.
   - We all talked a lot about how much we enjoy direct contact with both students and teachers.

   b. **What shifted in us during this conversation?**
   - We started paying a lot more attention to what our colleagues were saying toward the end.
   - There seemed to be a lot more emotional connection toward the end of the conversation.

   c. **What happened to our energy level as we discussed these questions?**
   - There seemed to be a lot of answers toward the beginning.
   - Everyone had a lot to say at the beginning. Things became really quiet in the middle. It seemed as though people had a hard time speaking.
   - Toward the end while we were quiet and serious, people were smiling and nodding heads. There was a lot of appreciation at the end.

Instructions

1. Lead the group through each of the following questions. Solicit several responses for each question. (The earlier questions are easier and may generate more responses than the later questions.)

   a. What tasks take up a lot of your time?

   b. Which of these tasks are a worthwhile use of your time? What would you like to spend your time doing?

   c. Which of these tasks are not a worthwhile use of your time? What would you rather *not* spend time doing?

   d. In what moments are you most discouraged? At what points are you ready to give up?

   e. What do you tell yourself that helps you continue? What do you do for yourself that helps you go on?

2. Process the discussion with one or two of the following questions:

   a. How was the group affected by this discussion?

   b. What shifted in us during this conversation?

   c. What happened to our energy level as we discussed these questions?

Possible Uses

The conductor uses this tool with groups that have lost their energy and are ready to bail out. The tool is helpful when the group sees no reason to move ahead. This conversation can also be used when the group members feel so overwhelmed that they bristle at the possibility of doing one more task.

Case Study

Finding Possibilities in the Real Situation

A school was required to carry out a planning process so that it might continue to receive funding for its Title I program. The staff began the process by doing a needs assessment. They gathered as much data as possible about their situation. They compiled and studied recent test scores, attendance figures, referrals for reading and math programs, parent participation, community economic figures, etc. The conductor (facilitator) created a standard format to help teams gather data and report the data to the group.

Unfortunately, the data was not encouraging. It indicated that they were located in an economically, socially, and culturally depressed area.

The conductor encouraged the teams to study the material and discuss the data. Slowly, the teams created a realistic profile of their community, their school, and their classrooms. The conductor then led them to create some focused directions that would make a difference for the whole school.

Working together, studying the facts and information, and creating a school focus created astounding confidence and hope. By studying the real situation first, the teams were able to devise and carry out solutions that made sense. The principal was ecstatic that many teachers began to voice the same possibilities he had talked about for years.

Chapter 11

The Concertmaster Harmonizes the Environment

The Concertmaster is the Group Energizer who focuses on shared decision-making.

Role Description

The concertmaster works with school teams to create a harmonious work environment. Organizational environments can either increase energy—encouraging people to work beyond quitting time—or cause burnout—driving people home early. "Individuals are self-motivated to achieve institutional objectives unless blocked by the organizational environment" (Astuto et al. 1994, p. 50). Most people desire to work hard and strive for fullfillment in their work (Astuto et al. 1994).

The concertmaster creates a work environment that fosters individual responsibility and recognizes genuine achievements to motivate educators (Astuto et al. 1994). "Success experiences and . . . environmental encouragement of change efforts . . . lead people to believe that their actions can make a difference" (Miles and Louis 1990, p. 58). She promotes a flexible schedule so educators can implement changes and meet with others. She allows all to share in making decisions and gives them the power to act on their decisions. She promotes teamwork, so team members can encourage and motivate one

another. Finally, she directs educators to focus on intrinsic motivation rather than extrinsic rewards.

Promoting Flexible Structures

The concertmaster promotes flexibility in scheduling to improve organizational structures. She creates dynamic and flexible structures so that teachers have time to initiate and implement innovative strategies that improve student learning and achievement (Astuto et al. 1994). She also provides time for teachers to support one another in their school change efforts.

> The importance of time cannot be overemphasized in the transitional process (Apps 1991). Transition to a new paradigm—a new way of perceiving, believing, and acting—takes place over time. Participants need opportunities to internalize, question, integrate, reframe, reorient, and test these new and innovative ways of perceiving, believing and acting. (Gallegos 1994, p. 36)

Participants also need time to confer, deliberate, choose, plan, and implement (Maeroff 1993 and Simpson 1990).

The concertmaster reforms schools that are traditionally constrictive, bureaucratic, and inflexible. She steers school administrators from focusing solely on consistency and efficiency to refocus on the botttom-line task of improving teaching and learning. She encourages teams to remodel the rigid, inflexible schedule early in the change process, before it becomes a major stumbling block on the road to change.

The concertmaster leads schools to seek creative ways to carve out more time for planning, discussing, and implementing. Some schools choose to extend instructional time by a few minutes each day, bank this time, and use it for half-day workshops or planning sessions. Other schools hire community people to teach extension courses while teachers meet. Some schools modify internal schedules, scheduling periods for teachers to meet. The concertmaster encourages schools to find solutions to the time dilemma that fit within their limitations and constraints.

Sharing Decision-Making Power

"Trusting people to solve problems generates higher levels of motivation and better solutions" (Bolman and Deal 1995, p. 106). The concertmaster encourages school leaders to trust their staff. When they trust their staff, leaders communicate a willingness to share power. They allow those most affected by particular issues to deal with those issues. When leaders share power, they literally share energy (Bolman and Deal 1995). Shared power can translate anger or despair into productive innovations and positive efforts toward change.

The concertmaster believes in ownership—all participants contributing to the change process. "Ownership describes personal links to the organization, the charged, emotion-driven feeling that can inspire people" (Wheatley 1992, p. 66). Ownership helps educators move beyond working solely for their paychecks to experiencing the energizing affects of wholeheartedly committing themselves to their jobs.

The concertmaster succeeds when educators begin to trust one another, to feel vitally connected to their work, and to participate actively in making decisions. As educators experience these things, the work of school change energizes them to press on.

Promoting Teamwork

Effective teams or cadres are the key to school change efforts. "The synergy gained through cooperation may accomplish for the school what never could be achieved by individuals working independently" (Maeroff 1993, p. 517). "The cadre is the facilitator of the transformation: learning, instructing, nurturing, and supporting individual, school, and district initiatives" (Joyce, Wolf, and Calhoun 1993, p. 42).

Teamwork does not automatically happen. The concertmaster spends time building and nurturing teams. She builds teams by allowing time for team sharing. As team members share with one another, they form strong bonds (Maeroff 1993). "The team grows stronger as its members recognize and acknowledge one another's strengths and empathize with one another's concerns" (Maeroff 1993, p. 517).

The concertmaster helps teams construct internal structures that continually renew their energy. She encourages relationship-building among team members, because quality relationships generate ideas as well as energy (Wheatley 1992). When team energy is released, productivity and performance increase. As productivity and performance increase, more energy is released.

The concertmaster recognizes that teams gain energy when they are given the responsibility and the power not only to make decisions but also to carry them out (Byham 1992). She encourages administrators to turn their advisory committees into implementation teams. Implementation teams coordinate with other teams to gather information, to create a change model, to share the model, and to implement the model; they are also held accountable for the results. Such responsibility calls forth energy even in the midst of demanding circumstances.

Fostering Instrinsic Motivation

The concertmaster's final task in harmonizing the work environment is fostering intrinsic motivation in every educator. Many leaders avoid improving the organizational environment because they find it easier to focus on extrinsic rewards, such as salaries, bonuses, and perks. Competitive, combative, confrontational organizational structures cause educators to focus on extrinsic rewards instead of job fulfillment. But extrinsic rewards do not generate genuine motivation for work (Astuto et al. 1994).

The concertmaster knows that the key to intrinsic motivation is helping people get in touch with their hopes and yearnings (Wheatley 1992). All people long for community, meaning, dignity, and love, but most don't realize that these longings can be fulfilled in the workplace. A workplace that does not tie in to people's longings for community, meaning, dignity, and love will be driven by extrinsic rewards alone.

The concertmaster seeks to bring the spiritual dimension back into the workplace.

> Modern managers concentrate mostly on the rational side of enterprise. Neglecting the spiritual dimension they overlook a powerful untapped source of energy and vitality. The costs of this omission are obscured by their deep devotion to the myth that reason can solve all problems. (Bolman and Deal 1995)

Looking at the workplace only through the eyes of logic and reason provides a one-dimensional view of reality. The concertmaster seeks to provide a three-dimensional approach by encouraging intuition and creativity. As people reach for creative, soulful solutions, they tap their inner resources of hope and energy. People who are in touch with this spiritual part of themselves can connect with others in a profound way.

The concertmaster helps people access their spiritual longings through "expressive activities" such as poetry, literature, music, art, theater, and dance (Bolman and Deal 1995).

> Expressive activity is integral to meaningful human enterprise. Its absence kills faith and hope. People put in time without passion or purpose. (Bolman and Deal 1995, p. 141)

The concertmaster chooses activities that highlight the significance of work and the workplace. In most workplaces, creative activities rarely happen. The concertmaster uses expressive activities that communicate the deep significance of the work being performed. She sponsors events to create links and bonds among people. She plans periodic events—featuring song, dance, drama,

art, or stories—that feed human motivation. As teams mature, expressive activities become part of their natural function, and they integrate such activities smoothly and gracefully into the life and flow of the school.

When This Role Is Needed

The change facilitator adopts this role when the organizational structure needs to be examined, polished, revamped, or refocused. The concertmaster creates the necessary time and opportunity to study the situation and how it can be improved. The concertmaster steps in when educators become focused on extrinsic rewards, when they leave work early or are only focused on getting their paycheck, rather than intrinsic motivations. This role is also needed when motivation lags and energy drops.

Skills

The concertmaster creates a humanizing work environment. She knows how to find time for school change efforts. She is skilled in sharing responsibility, accountability, decision-making, and power with the team. She helps teams develop trust and commitment. The concertmaster also is skilled in creating "expressive activities" that generate enthusiasm and a deep connection to the internal motivations of those involved.

Practical Tools

The concertmaster can use the following practical tools to assist her in creating a harmonious work environment:

1. "What's the Real Enemy?" Activity
2. Energy Clues and Occasions of Energy Chart
3. Human Structures/Motivating Environment Screen
4. Showcase the Story Activity

Practical Tool 1
"What's the Real Enemy?" Activity

Description

This tool helps the team locate the real enemy within the system or structure rather than blame an individual or group for systemic problems.

Example

What happened? What are the facts and details behind the event?

Community voted down a proposal for school levy (vote was 61/39 against)

Neighborhoods with senior citizens voted against the levy

Newspaper encouraged a vote for levy

Several letters to the editor against levy

Chamber of Commerce supported levy

How did we react to this problem?

What are our reactions and emotions?

Angry and disappointed

We thought we had won this time.

What would a more helpful or encouraging structure or system look like?

A school interconnected with many parts of the community

A school that serves all ages, all generations of the community

What steps can we take to move toward such a structure?

(1) Student community service project

(2) Business, parent, senior citizen, community connections to students and the classroom

(3) Student apprenticeships in businesses

(4) Teachers and high school students offering classes to community

Outside of families with school age children the community is disconnected from schools.

Most of the community feels no personal benefit from the school.

Education seems to be a low priority.

Community doesn't value our role as teachers.

A levy for a sports stadium passed.

What is the structural or systemic enemy?

What are we really upset or angry about?

Instructions

Note: A blackline master of the "What's the Real Enemy?" Chart is provided in Appendix A, page 204.

1. Lead the group through all of the questions on the chart in the following order:

   a. What happened? What are the facts and details behind the event? Ask the team to explain what happened and to supply as many details as they can.

   b. How did we react to this problem? Give the group time to air all of their feelings about the issue.

   c. What are we really upset or angry about? Encourage the team to name events or details that really upset or angered them.

   d. What is the the structural or systemic enemy? or What is the real enemy? Push the group to find the systemic enemy, rather than focus on a personal or superfluous problem.

   e. What would a more helpful or encouraging structure or system look like? Push the group to name some positive structural or systemic changes.

   f. What steps can we take to move toward such a structure? Give the group time to devise a step-by-step process to improve the structure or system.

2. Conclude by asking some processing questions such as the following:

   a. What was helpful for us in this activity?

   b. How has our perspective been altered?

   c. What learnings about implementing change do we have now?

Possible Uses

This activity is especially crucial when teams begin to blame an individual or a group for its struggles. For example, a group may say, "This happened because the principal never supported us"; "This happened because no one in the administrative office understands what we are doing here"; or "The Board never wants to try anything new." When teams move to thinking structurally, it can devise implementation steps to overcome particular personalities and to impact structural problems.

Practical Tool 2
Energy Clues and
Occasions of Energy Chart

Description

This tool helps a team discern its energy level and decide what type of activity will improve it. It also provides teams with some ideas for energy-enhancing activities.

Example

Energy Clues	
Expressing Energy Activities	**Inviting Quick Energy Activities**
• The team has been engaged on a long-term project that hasn't produced any concrete or visible wins yet. • The team has many creative team members. • Teams have not gathered as a whole group for awhile.	• The team is usually perky but recently displays signs of decreasing energy. • The team has just been through one or two weeks of unusually hard work and team members are worn out. • The team has run into a small obstacle and team members feel they have had "the wind knocked out of them."
Honoring Energy Activities	**Generating Massive Energy Activities**
• The team feels certain that no one knows how hard they are working. • The team has been working for months and months without a celebration or recognition of its labors. • The team has produced a string of successes.	• The team experienced a massive setback. • Many team members wonder why they signed up in the first place. • Members who have recently joined the team do not understand the big picture.

Instructions

Note: A blackline master of Energy Clues is provided in Appendix A, page 205.

1. Pull out this tool when a team's energy is lagging.

2. Encourage the team to look at the Energy Clues blackline to discern what kind of energy activity they need at this point.

3. Share the following chart with the group. Ask the group to pick an activity idea from one of the four categories.

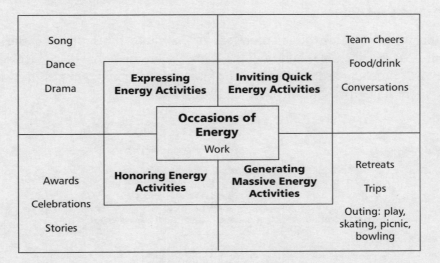

4. Allow the team time to plan an activity and choose a date to hold it. If appropriate, the team may choose to do the activity within the meeting time.

5. Follow up after the activity with a short conversation. You may ask the following questions or choose your own questions.

   a. What do you remember about what happened?

   b. What did you like about what happened?

   c. What did it do for us as a team?

   d. What other activities might we do sometime?

Possible Uses

The concertmaster pulls out this tool when she notices that team members are dragging to meetings, complaining about difficult tasks, commenting that school change never ends, or are upset by things that never bothered them before. This activity allows team members to be aware of the team mood and demonstrates to them that mood swings are legitimate and natural. It also suggests that there are ways to spark new energy. Newly formed teams may find it difficult to discern their mood, but as teams mature they will find it easier to recognize mood changes.

Practical Tool 3
Human Structures/Motivating Environment Screen

Description

This tool provides teams with a framework for examining three aspects of the school system—the district, the school, and the teams. Teams discern what aspects of their work environment are supportive and encouraging and brainstorm possible ways to create more supportive and encouraging structures.

Example

District
1. Night to showcase each school's accomplishing of district goals
2. Creating videos of each school
3. Articles in the local paper featuring schools and teachers
4. Invite other districts to see what is happening
5. Formulate a small number of district goals or district focuses
6. Hold community/parent events to keep them informed about new approaches to learning
7. Make school plans that expand and carry out the limited number of district goals

School
1. Teachers-Who-Risk Awards
2. School-aims retreat
3. Faculty meetings include 15 minutes for sharing victories and task force reports
4. Teachers choose professional goals and are evaluated according to these goals
5. Space and time provided for team meetings
6. Task forces designated to devise solution models
7. One major emphasis for a year
8. Faculty meetings feature the innovations
9. Principals spend time increasing teachers' instructional prowess
10. Create site-based management or shared decision-making teams
11. Emphasize data collection to document needs and progress
12. Encourage teachers to do action research projects in innovative methods

Teams
1. Short, concise meetings (begin and end on time)
2. Regular meeting times
3. Each meeting has a clear focus and produces a definitive product
4. Consistent team meeting space—even if shared with other teams
5. Rotating leadership assignments
6. Task assignments written, published, and shared
7. Check-in conversations about how things are going, what is being learned, etc.

Instructions

Note: A blackline master of the Human Structures/Motivating Environment Screen is provided in Appendix A, page 206.

1. Divide the group into three teams and assign each to focus on one of the following: district, school, or teams.

2. Instruct teams to decide what supportive and encouraging structures or aspects currently exist within their assigned environment.

3. Ask teams to share their observations. Write these ideas on a Human Structures/Motivating Environment Screen displayed in the front of the room or on an overhead projecter. After each team has reported, ask the whole group for any additions.

4. Lead teams to brainstorm new structures that would increase support and encouragement in their assigned environment.

5. Ask teams to share their observations. Write these ideas on a chart in the front of the room. After each team has reported, ask the whole group for any additions.

6. Invite teams to focus on one or two of their ideas and to devise tactics or steps for putting the ideas into place.

7. Agree with team members to follow up this work at a future meeting. Teams may want to set a deadline for implementation.

8. Process this activity with one or more of the following questions:

   a. What suggestions had you never considered before?

   b. What happened in this activity that surprised you?

   c. How has your thinking about structures and environments shifted during this activity?

   d. What would happen if some of the ideas were implemented?

Possible Uses

At the outset of any major shift in direction, teams can use this tool to consider how to restructure the work environment so that it supports and encourages change. This activity is especially useful if the innovation is to be considered more seriously than the latest fad. This activity helps teams move innovations from initiation to incorporation.

Practical Tool 4
Showcase the Story Activity

Description

This expressive activity helps a team to discover its story, to write the story, and to enact the story. The story articulates past accomplishments, current challenges, and future victories. (This tool is modified from *More Than 50 Ways to Build Team Consensus* by R. Bruce Williams [1993, pp. 197–199].)

Example

Our Story

Our Past Accomplishments
Highland Fields High School has an eighty year history of noteworthy accomplishments. Our high school has a reputation for achievements in academics and sports. More than 70 percent of our students have gone on to college. Our debate team has often received regional and state honors. The football team has often won the state championship. We are pleased that families moving into this county often decide to send their teenagers to our school.

Our Current Challenges
Highland Fields High School is going through many changes. In the last five years, standardized test scores have dropped. The dropout rate has doubled. Attendance has decreased from 95 percent to 88 percent. Discipline issues have increased three-fold in the last three years. While changing demographics have brought a much more diverse student population, dropouts, truancy, and discipline issues are increasing in all segments of the student population. To meet these challenges, the teachers are participating in professional development opportunities to expand their instructional strategies. While it is too early to see conclusive statistics, there are some encouraging signs. In addition, teachers are organized into cross-departmental teams to work on whole school concerns and issues.

Our Future Victories
Highland Fields High School is committed to encouraging all of its students to pursue some form of post secondary education or training. This training might include university, college, community college, trade school, or any other additional training. To that end, the school is initiating a block scheduling format to help students focus their class time as well as to help students better connect their learning through integrated, interdisciplinary approaches to curriculum. Highland Fields High School is committed to increasing the academic achievement of all its students as its bottom-line responsibility to the community. Our community is taking this challenge so seriously that it has matched our high school's commitment with both financial and human resources. This unqualified participation and involvement of both individuals and community organizations is paving the way to an exciting new future for Highland Fields High School.

Instructions

1. Set out materials such as chart paper, markers, masking tape, pencil, and paper.

2. Set the stage by saying a few words about the role of winning stories. You might ask the group:

   a. What successful teams have you been a part of?

   b. What do you imagine were the stories these teams had about themselves that helped them to win?

3. With the group, brainstorm ideas for the story in each of these three areas:

The Past	The Present	The Future
What has happened?	What is going on now?	Where are we heading?
Our past accomplishments	Our current challenges	Our future victories

4. Divide the group into three teams. Assign one team to each of the three sections—past, present, and future. Allow teams ten to fifteen minutes to write a paragraph on their assigned section. Suggest that teams write their paragraphs on chart paper, large enough to display to the whole group.

5. Ask representatives from each team to read their paragraphs. Applaud after the whole story is read.

6. Reassemble teams. Allow teams 15 minutes to devise an "expressive" way to represent their section (e.g., dance, pantomine, skit, song).

7. Have each team offer its presentation.

8. Conclude with some processing questions, such as the following:

   a. What do you recall from the stories and the presentations?

   b. What was the highlight of the stories and the presentations for you?

   c. What were some of the underlying messages communicated about our team and our school?

   d. Did the presentations change your viewpoint of the stories?

Possible Uses

This tool can be used to celebrate a completed phase of implementation or the end of a school year. This activity can be tremendously healing as humor can override the mention of difficult times. This activity can also be a motivating prelude to looking ahead and doing concrete planning for the next implementation period or the next school year.

Case Study

Creating More Human Environments

Schools and teachers around the country are devising simple shifts and complex changes to alter their work environments. Concertmasters (facilitators) have helped them devise ingenious plans that make significant impacts. The following are some simple changes that have had large impacts on the school environment.

One school felt that the students were not identifying with the teachers—the teachers seemed distant to the students. This faculty decided to put on periodic skits and songfests for the whole student body. The teachers created skits and songs that spoke to the students and fit the situations within the school. The students began to see the teachers in a new light. The environment opened and brightened.

Another school felt that staff members were disconnected and isolated from each other. The concertmaster worked with the staff to form a "secret buddy" system. The secret buddy sent cards or small gifts to her buddy on her birthday, on holidays, or for other special occassions. This system created a mood of excitement and anticipation. Staff members connected with one another in new ways as the secret buddies sent creative surprises throughout the year.

Finally, a school recognized that some students naturally received much attention while others received almost none. To alleviate the problem, teachers began to stand outside their rooms in the morning, greeting students from their classes and other classess as they walked down the hall. Needless to say, they paid particular attention to the students whom they felt needed extra care. This simple action created a more alive, brighter atmosphere throughout the school.

Chapter 12

The Critic Celebrates the Performance

The Critic is the Group Energizer who focuses on communicating visible achievements.

Role Description

The critic celebrates the team's performance, allowing the team to gain energy from its own accomplishments. He embodies optimism when team members feel discouraged. He highlights victories when a team feels overwhelmed by losses and failures. He asks questions that aid the team in assessing its strengths, skills, and accomplishments. He guides teams to set benchmarks for success at the beginning of a venture, so the team can measure its success along the way. The critic encourages voices from outside the team to note the team's successes and victories so that encouragement continues both internally and externally.

Gathering Data

Daily struggles, endless tasks, and challenging obstacles can drain energy from a school change team; the team may begin to feel it is losing the battle. In most cases, the team is making progress, but it has not developed a way to measure advances. Hard data can reveal how much progress the team has made.

The critic pushes the team to gather concrete information and data on its performance. He enables the team to discern what it can measure, how it can assess its present situation, how it will measure ongoing progress, and how it will use data to make future plans. Information that is presented objectively and clearly not only convinces others that the team is advancing, but it also convinces the team.

As time goes on and as the tasks stretch out, team members may lose their energy and desire. Incontrovertible evidence and documentation can keep participants clearly focused on real accomplishments. Evidence of advancement can encourage and motivate the team to tackle more complex projects or to begin new tasks.

Data can also be used to demonstrate to other teachers and community members what is working and what is not working. The critic helps teams target and accumulate data that bears accurate, understandable evidence—inaccurate or inconclusive data is useless.

For example, many teachers feel that standardized tests don't correctly measure what their students know. The critic would challenge these teachers to devise more accurate measures so that they "could see what was happening in their classrooms and then determine if their continuous improvement ideas were effective" (Byham 1992, p. 233).

Gathering evidence about the impact of teaching strategies and approaches puts educators in the role of action researchers. As disciplined researchers, educators welcome information, because information directs them in how to proceed.

Note: To learn more about data gathering tools, consult The Memory Jogger *by Michael Brassard and Diane Ritter (1994). This booklet includes charts, forms, images, and graphs that help educators gather, interpret, and present data.*

Spotlighting Accomplishments

When educators gather, they typically share their struggles and frustrations—what's wrong with the school system, what's not working in the classroom, what student is failing or misbehaving. The critic steers educators to talk about what *is* working and winning. He does not ignore struggles and setbacks or proclaim false or unsubstantiated victories (false victories create as much cynicism as negative conversation). Instead, he proclaims proven accomplishments.

Teams that focus on real, documentable accomplishments become empowered and motivated.

> Empowerment is the engine that moves people along on this road. People are motivated to make continuous improvements because they enjoy the sense of pride they obtain from their accomplishments. (Byham 1992, p. viii)

The critic invests time in highlighting the team's accomplishments. As teams focus on achievements, they begin to change their internal stories about themselves as educators, about the school system, and about the future of education.

Many educators are gripped by failure. National and local news reports proclaim that schools are failing. Yet there are miraculous things happening in schools and districts across the country. The critic urges teams to combat negative media by featuring and proclaiming good news. Teams can feature their successes in faculty meetings, press releases, newsletters, and school open houses. As the community notices positive changes, negativity disappears.

Creating Stories

The critic takes teams beyond reporting accomplishments to creating epic narratives. Facts and details are crucial because they demonstrate that progress is documentable, but creating a story helps team members connect with their deeper motivations.

> Stories take us to other worlds. They transport us to the world of spirit. (Bolman and Deal 1995, p. 98)

The story returns team members to the source of their motivation and to the power that profoundly connects them to their colleagues. Mere facts and data cannot do this. "Throughout history, people have relied on narrative to express deep spiritual messages hard to communicate any other way" (Bolman and Deal 1995 p. 142).

The critic encourages the team to craft a story from the data it has gathered. A story transforms a simple happening into a significant, meaningful event. It breathes emotion and humanity into the facts and details. It applauds the heroines and the heroes. It transforms struggles and obstacles into meaningful learnings and insights within a context of victory.

As team members write and review their stories, they experience renewed enthusiasm for the tasks ahead. They become eager to move on to the next chapter.

When This Role Is Needed

This role becomes crucial when implementers realize that they are engaged in a long-term task and lose their initial enthusiasm for change. The critic steps in when everyone turns up sick or team members become preoccupied with concerns outside of their tasks. The critic refocuses teams by revealing evidence of success and by illuminating how the data and the story point to the next step.

Skills

The critic draws energy from a team's visible victories. He is especially skilled in interpreting data, gathering evidence of victories, and creating documentation about successes. The critic is persistent in amassing crucial facts and creative in presenting understandable reports and demonstrations. Finally, the critic is a master storyteller. He weaves objective data into a powerful narrative that communicates the dramatic shifts and numerous victories occurring in the journey to school transformation.

Practical Tools

The critic uses the following practical tools to celebrate the team's performance:

1. Data Gathering Conversation
2 Accomplishments-Pride-Empowerment Conversation
3. School Portfolio
4. Structure of a Story

Practical Tool 1
Data Gathering Conversation

Description

This tool helps the group extract meaning from data assembled from some kind of graphics tool. (*The Memory Jogger* by Michael Brassard and Diane Ritter [1994] offers a variety of graphic tools.) It leads a group to discuss possible connections, relationships, and next steps.

Example

Data Gathering Questions

1. **What facts, data, and other information are you noticing as you read and study this tool?**
   - There is a significant difference in the percentage of referrals (to the principal and guidance counselor) in the last two years compared with the referrals this year.
   - There was a decrease in absences this year.
   - I'm surprised at how much the test scores rose from last year to this year.
   - According to these figures, our students made great strides in science.

2. **What connections and relationships are you discerning as you continue to study this tool?**
   - For some reason, our move to block scheduling is encouraging students to be absent less often.
   - Our team teaching in multiage classroom has cut down the number of referrals we have made to the principal and the guidance counselor.
   - The new science curriculum has had great results.

3. **What messages is this information communicating to us?**
   - It takes awhile for our teachers to get on top of new curriculum, but once they do we start seeing results.
   - The effort our teachers are making in varying instructional strategies and using different resources in the classroom is cutting down our discipline issues.

4. **What is this telling us about what we are doing well? or What is this telling us about where our wins and victories are?**
   - According to these figures, we are showing the most progress in the places where our teachers have been risking the most with new approaches.
   - These also tell us that we were right not to get discouraged last year when we didn't see immediate results.
   - Many of our teachers who have always done well throught the years are continuing to do well, but their students are not showing leaps in improvement.

5. **What are our next steps? What do we need to keep doing? What do we need to change?**
   - We need to do the same curriculum changes in math that we have been doing in science.
   - We need to get some feedback from the students to see if they are experiencing the same positive results we are.
   - The students' feedback could also guide some of our next changes.

Instructions

Note: A blackline master of the Data Gathering Questions is provided in Appendix A, page 207.

1. Distribute copies or make a poster of the information compiled in a previous data-gathering activity. (For data-gathering tools, see *The Memory Jogger* [Brassard and Ritter 1994]. This booklet includes numerous charts, forms, images, and graphs that help educators gather, interpret, and present data.)

2. Divide the group into teams of two or three. Give each team a copy of the Data Gathering Conversation. Give teams time to discuss the questions.

3. Gather the whole group for discussion. Discuss each question, getting input from each team.

4. Record answers to question 5 on chart paper. Direct the group to spell out the next steps. Plans should include who will be involved, what will happen, and when it will happen.

5. Process this activity with the following questions:

   a. What happened to us as we studied and worked on the data gathering tool?

   b. What was effective about the tool?

   c. What worked in the conversation that we had?

   d. How has this information affected your sense about our effectiveness as a staff?

   e. What have we learned about the role of hard data?

Possible Uses

The critic can use this tool to convince cynics that strategies are working and change is happening. The conversation generates positive and insightful comments about data. It uses the combined power of many minds to discern and articulate what the data reveals. This tool has the power to shift mindsets, even if the shift is no greater than a "Well, I'd like to try this little piece and see if it works in my classroom."

Practical Tool 2
Accomplishments-Pride-Empowerment Conversation

Description

The questionnaire and conversation help educators think about the impact accomplishments are having in the school. It allows educators to reflect on how the accomplishments have excited them, changed them, and empowered them.

Example

Accomplishments Questionnaire

1. **Name some of your projects or accomplishments from the past three months, six months, or year.**
   - Interdisciplinary unit on space
   - Initiation of the peer tutoring program
   - Team teaching occurring at some point in each grade level
   - Portfolio Night
   - Health Fair

2. **What projects or accomplishments have pleased or excited you the most?**
   - My unit on elections
   - Team teaching with the music teacher and the special ed teacher
   - How Rose and Ben responded to the peer tutoring program
   - Enthusiasm of the bank employees as they came every week to our class

3. **How have these impacted your image of yourself as a teacher? What difference are these accomplishments making in your belief in the kind of teacher you are?**
   - I'm starting to believe again that there are ways to help each student learn.
   - My confidence is returning as community people have complimented me on my teaching skills while they worked with me on the last two units.
   - By using some of the new instructional strategies, I see students getting excited who have never been excited before. This is reminding me why I decided to go into teaching.
   - I am beginning to be more comfortable in some aspects of the facilitating role.

4. **What are you ready to tackle now that maybe you weren't ready to tackle a year ago?**
   - I have been so afraid of dealing with computers. Now that I have met some key community people who are good at computers and now that I have seen

---

(Continued on next page)

how skilled some of my students are I am ready to increase the use of technology in my units.

- Until now all of you know I haven't been willing to try any of the cooperative strategies in my classroom. However, when I saw the work that some of my students from last year accomplished because they were working in teams, I am ready to ask for some help in getting started in this.
- Mrs. Santos and I have decided we are going to write for that grant we've been talking about. We were amazed at what Mr. Kim did in his classes with the grant he wrote for and received.

5. What's happening to us as an entire staff? How are we changing?

- I notice a huge difference in the lunchroom conversations. They are more lively and almost always seem to be about what surprising and encouraging things are starting to happen.
- More individuals in our implementation teams are willingly volunteering to carry out more of our projects.
- The students seem to be reacting differently. They come to classes much more focused and ready to work. They even come up to teachers asking more questions about the content. They used to run out of class as fast as they could

Instructions

Note: A blackline master of the Accomplishments Questionnaire is provided in Appendix A, page 208.

1. Direct individuals to spend ten minutes to complete the Accomplishments Questionnaire.

2. Lead the group through each of the five questions on the questionnaire. Solicit several responses for each question. (The earlier questions are easier and may generate more responses than the later questions.)

3. Ask one or two of these processing questions:

   a. What happend to your thinking as you worked on the questionnaire?

   b. What did you notice going on in the group as we held our conversation?

   c. Why is it important for us to focus on our accomplishments like this?

Possible Uses

This tool can be used to reflect on accomplishments at the end of the year or when a task is completed. The critic uses the tool when he discovers that the group's energy is waning or enthusiasm has decreased. This conversation is very appropriate for groups that have been working together for awhile and can trust one another enough to engage in a conversation that is internally focused.

Practical Tool 3
School Portfolio

Description

A portfolio provides tangible proof of victories. The school portfolio is a collection of evidence displaying real, identifiable accomplishments and events in the life of the school. This tool helps the team to determine what will go into the school portfolio.

Example

Arena / Grade Level	Student Learning	Collegial Teamwork	Parent/Community Connections
K	Examples or pictures of student projects	Interdisciplinary unit plans	Parent newsletters
1	Graph of rise in test scores	Team teaching events	Increased outside agency connections
2	Student-written books	Peer coaching schedule	Graph of rise in volunteers
3	Student portfolios	Schedule of common planning times	Pictures of student service projects
4	Student problem-solving journals	Graph of reduced discipline referrals	Report on student apprenticeship program

Our School Portfolio

Instructions

Note: A blackline master of Our School Portfolio is provided in Appendix A, page 209.

1. Lead the group to name categories (e.g., goals or emphases) that the portfolio will be organized around.

2. Encourage all teachers and staff to contribute items to the portfolio as the year progresses.

3. From time to time, spend a few minutes in staff meetings to highlight some of the contents of the school portfolio.

4. At the end of the school year, allow teacher teams to examine their contributions and choose their best work. Include only the best items in the final

portfolio. (Teams may review the contributions of other teams and make suggestions on which to retain.)

5. When the final portfolio is complete, discuss these questions with the group:

   a. What items from the portfolio do you best remember?

   b. Which items pleased or surprised you?

   c. What does the portfolio reveal about what our school has accomplished this year?

   d. How have attitudes and procedures changed from where we were last year to where we are now?

   e. Considering what we have learned from this portfolio, what should our next steps be?

Possible Uses

This tool is a great way to show the central administration or other schools what has been going on in a particular school. The portfolio can be shown to parents, current students, prospective students, or media representatives. The portfolio can also impact the school staff—driving away cynicism and despair with documented proof of accomplishments.

Practical Tool 4
Structure of a Story

Description

For people who don't know how to write a story, this tool offers some simple guide-lines. Teams use the story chart and a brainstorming activity to determine what will be included in their story.

Example

Create A Story Chart		
Setting	**Heroes/Heroines**	**Villains**
Elementary school Teachers have had a great deal of staff development in varied instructional approaches and new ways of assessment. Teachers have guided students all year in gathering material for portfolio Using teacher teams	Each student Teachers	Negative comments Competing events Conflicting priorities
Conflict	**Resolution**	**Ending**
No plan 3 weeks before event How to get parents to see students' work	The event Guide sheet Time breakdown Children's personal invitation	Debriefing meeting Stories Assistant superintendant letter and comments

---

Sample Story

(Beginning)
Once upon a time, there was a school in a diverse, suburban community filled with hard-working teachers and students struggling to met the challenges of learning in the late twentieth century. The teachers under the able leadership of their forward-thinking principal had participated in several training events and acquired numerous skills in alternative instructional strategies such as cooperative learning, multiple intelligences, and critical thinking. Several teachers worked in teaching teams in multiage settings. The students worked all year on projects, journals, creative writing, and art work. The teachers guided the students in putting their work into portfolios. The teachers

Continued on next page

dreamed of holding a night to show off students' work to their parents. Unfortunately, three monster dragons were looming between the teachers and the students and the realization of the teachers' dream. The monster dragons were Competing Events, Conflicting Priorities, and Negative Comments.

(Middle)
Three weeks before the dream was to be realized, the staff huddled to plan for how they would conquer the dragons. They spoke in determined quiet voices so that the dragons would never hear their plan.

They decided to create traps to surprise each dragon. They figured if they could surprise the dragons, the dragons being so huge would not be able to react quickly enough.

They knew that families and students had many Competing Events that were eating up their time and would make it hard to attend. Some students even had sports events to participate in. So they decided to divide the evening into three time frames and invite people to attend only one of the time frames. As a guideline they broke the alphabet into threes and suggested families with last names beginning with A–H attend first, I–O attend second, and P–Z attend third.

Next, they created a trap for the dragon of Conflicting Priorities. Their plan included sending letters to parents, placing announcements in the newspaper and the PTA newsletter, and asking students to create and write personal invitations to their parents asking them to come or to send another adult to come in their place. These invitations went home a few days before the big night.

Finally, the teachers were concerned that parents would be confused by the portfolio format—students presenting their work to their parents—or that parents might make negative comments during the presentation. So the teachers created a portfolio presentation format complete with suggested appropriate comments and questions.

The teachers came up with additional ways to make the night successful. They invited high school students to care for the students' siblings so that parents could focus on their child's portfolio. The PTA hosted an ice cream

sundae buffet for parents to attend after the portfolio presentation. Student art work decorated the hallways.

The teachers also decided to make the students the stars of the night. The teachers agreed that their only role was to facilitate the portfolio presentations and to step in only when necessary. Before the presentations, teachers helped the students to practice their presentations in role plays.

As the night approached, teachers became more confident that the dragons would be caught off guard. The dragons were definitely accustomed to winning without any effort.

The big event happened. To everyone's surprise, 99 percent of the students had their parents or another significant adult present. The teachers had never experienced such participation by the parents. The students carried off their presentations with pride and delight. The parents showered the students with excitement and praise. Many parents said they had no idea their children were so capable. The ice cream sundae buffet created a wonderful celebration and acknowledgment of the students' achievements. As the evening progressed, one by one, sensing a massive defeat, each dragon wandered to find another school to menace.

(Conclusion)
A few days later, the teachers gathered once more to talk about the Portfolio Night and the success of their dream. This time their voices were strong and loud. They desired to announce their victory to whoever would listen. They were proud of the glowing letter that they received from the Assistant Superintendent. He not only commended the teachers, but proclaimed to the community the success of the Portfolio Night and the victory over the dragons. The teachers reported that indeed the students had shone as stars that night during the presentations and as they showed their artwork. Teachers reported that they had never seen such quiet purpose in the whole building. Parents knew what they were there for. Students were clear about their tasks. The teachers were confident in their preparations. A veteran teacher commented that the Portfolio Night was a highlight in her teaching career.

Instructions

Note: A blackline master of the Create a Story Chart is provided in Appendix A, page 210.

1. Ask the group to pick one accomplishment or victory to write a story about.

2. Display the Create a Story Chart. If the group has fewer than twelve people, ask the whole group to brainstorm items for each category. If the group has twelve or more people, divide the group into six teams. Assign each team to brainstorm items for one category. When teams finish brainstorming, ask them to share their ideas. Encourage others to offer additional ideas.

3. Record brainstormed ideas on the chart.

4. Direct participants to determine the flow of the story. Divide the story into three parts—beginning, middle, and the conclusion. Have the group brainstorm what to include in each section.

5. Divide the group into three teams, assigning one part to each team. Ask teams to write at least two paragraphs, including information from the story chart and from the brainstorming.

6. Ask teams to read their section aloud. Allow time for comments and reflections.

7. Request that two or three people volunteer to polish or edit the story and to type it up for everyone.

8. Choose some of these questions to process this experience:

   a. What parts of the story do you recall?

   b. What surprised you today about what we did?

   c. What happened to us as we heard this story?

   d. How will this story impact others?

Possible Uses

This tool is another good way to end a school year or wrap up an implementation step. Writing a story helps the implementation teams to focus on and review the past year. The critic could use this tool with teams from every school in the district so that schools may share their stories with one another. The key is how the format of the story captures the imaginations of and creates connections in the minds of the audience.

Case Study

Surprised by the Truth

A critic (facilitator) was working with a number of school teams helping them understand and process the data they had collected. One school was deeply concerned over the number of special-needs students assigned to the school and was convinced they needed more resources to help them. To this end, they brought all the information from their own school to create a chart of their total school population and the percentage of special-needs students they had.

Since they were working with teams from the other schools in the district, the critic suggested they add data from the other schools to their chart. This peaked their interest, so they quickly gathered the information to add to their chart.

They discovered that while they certainly had a high percentage of special-needs students, they did not have the largest percentage after all. When they realized that another school was in a similar situation, they approached the other school about how they might work together and help each other.

Their mood changed from "look at poor us" to sharing innovative ideas with the other school. Understanding the real situation represented by the data had transformed their attitudes. The critic helped them to see their real situation without having to "criticize" or "shove it down their throats." The data had helped them understand the truth about their situation and opened them up to new possibilities for creative solutions.

Epilogue

As the reader continues the task of facilitating school change, the author would welcome any additional comments, reflections, clarifications, and new insights.

The truth is, the more you understand about the details and the complexity of this work of school change, it would be possible to conclude that it all looks quite impossible. The stumbling blocks often appear larger than the possibilities. Yet, after Fullan's exhaustive study on schools implementing structural and systemic change, he remarks:

> The point of all this is that successful change is possible in the real world, even under difficult conditions. . . . there are classrooms, schools, communities, districts, and states that have altered the conditions for change in more favorable, workable directions. Not every situation is alterable, especially at certain periods of time; but it is a good bet that major improvements can be accomplished in many more settings than is happening at present. (1991, p. 102)

The facilitator who keeps the long-range goals and the short-range tasks focused on student learning and achievement, who keeps groups and teams focused on shared decision-making, and who keeps the communication and interaction focused on visible victories, can make the difference between an overwhelming and impossible task and a task that, while full of hard work, is not only fun but also continuously motivating.

Appendix A

Blacklines

The following blackline masters are for your use with your teams. You may copy them or create forms of your own.

Needs Assessment Grid

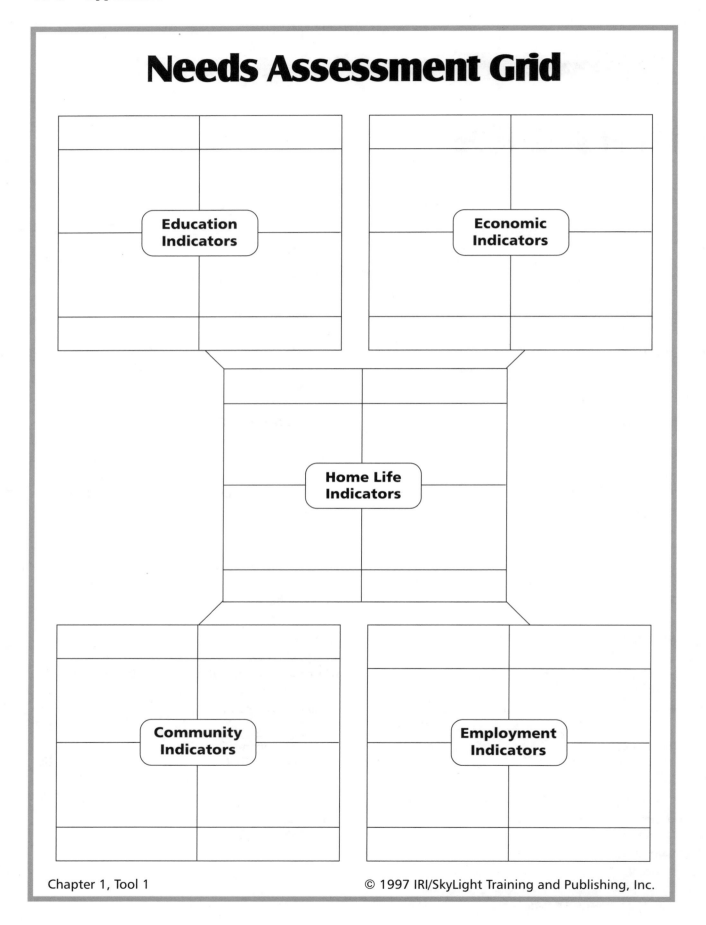

Education Indicators

Economic Indicators

Home Life Indicators

Community Indicators

Employment Indicators

Resource Analysis Chart

Title:	
Author's Key Ideas	
Crucial Insights	
Local Implication	

Visible Achievement Wheel

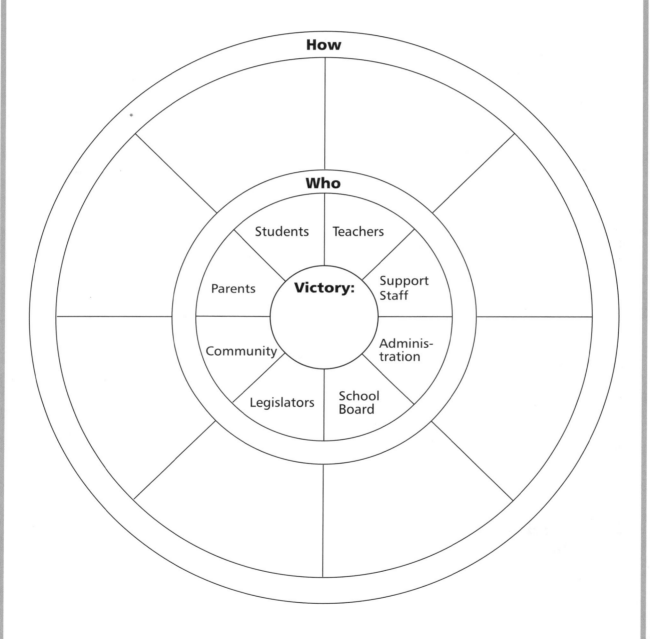

Cooperative Learning Lesson Plan

Name _____

Grade, Subject _____

Lesson Objective	Hook	Roles	Materials for students
			For teacher

Room Configuration, Type of Group, Number in Each Group	Task Directions (complete on back if more room needed)

BUILD in Higher Order Thinking	UNIFY the Teams	INSURE Individual Accountability	LOOK Over and Discuss	DEVELOP Social Skills

Applications

Three-Story Questions 1

Three Story—Applying

Two Story—Processing

One Story—Gathering

Three-Story Questions 2

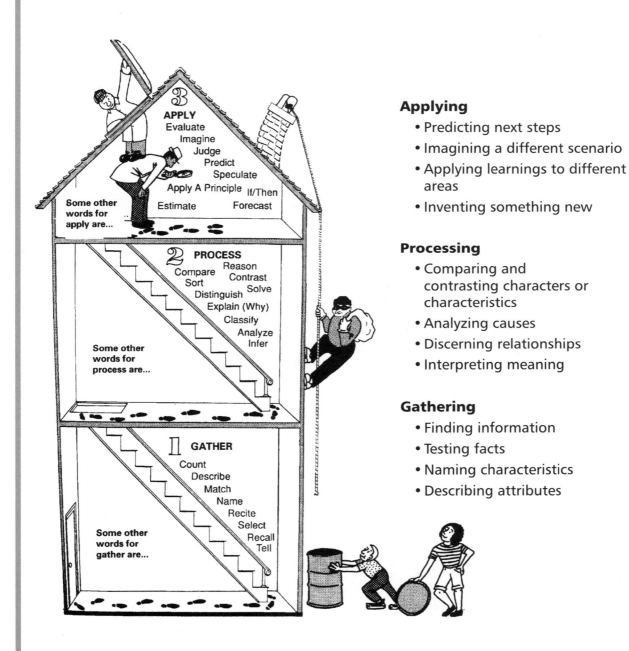

Applying
- Predicting next steps
- Imagining a different scenario
- Applying learnings to different areas
- Inventing something new

Processing
- Comparing and contrasting characters or characteristics
- Analyzing causes
- Discerning relationships
- Interpreting meaning

Gathering
- Finding information
- Testing facts
- Naming characteristics
- Describing attributes

Multiple Intelligences Unit Plan

Logical/Mathematical	Visual/Spatial	Verbal/Linguistic	Interpersonal
Musical/Rhythmic	Intrapersonal	Bodily/Kinesthetic	Naturalist

Teacher Self-Examination Guide

Criteria	Little	Some	A Lot
Criteria 1:			
Element 1: Element 2:			
Criteria 2:			
Element 1: Element 2:			
Criteria 3:			
Element 1: Element 2:			
Criteria 4:			
Element 1: Element 2:			

Chapter 4, Tool 5

My Résumé

Name:

Work Experience:

Education/Professional Development:

Skills/Expertise:

Hobbies/Talents:

Team Assessment Guide

CRITERIA	1	2	3	4
PURPOSEFUL VISION				
Overall Mission	Write and display	Referred to once a quarter	Connect to large team tasks	Verbally and visually connect to every team task
Specific Tasks	Some tasks seem mandated	Some tasks are overwhelming, others realistic	All tasks make sense	All tasks come from the group and connect to the overall mission
Documentation	Keep minutes	Keep quarterly plans and minutes	Keep and distribute quarterly plans and minutes to all	Keep and distribute quarterly plans, minutes, and meeting products to all
PARTICIPATIVE PROCESSES				
Leadership	Leadership works but never changes	Leadership highly effective but never shared	Effective leadership occasionally shared	Leadership rotated and information shared
Approaches	Sometimes one person controls	Input occasionally requested	Much input	Input directed and focused
Meetings	Start and end on time	Punctual; some tasks completed	Punctual; all tasks completed	Dynamic and punctual; all tasks completed
COLLABORATIVE TEAMS				
Working Relationships	Team members work with each other	Team members develop team cohesiveness	Team members support each other in tasks and differences	Team members take on each others' tasks when needed to complete team tasks
Roles	Individuals remain in the same roles	Roles rotated on a volunteer basis	Roles rotated according to a publicized plan	Roles rotated and periodically recreated and renamed
Recognitions/ Celebrations	Holiday parties	Birthday celebrations	Quarterly team victory celebrations	Frequent recognitions of team and individual accomplishments
INDIVIDUAL COMMITMENT				
Absence/Presence	More than 50% of the team present	More than 75% of the team present	Everyone usually present, some absences unexplained	Everyone usually present, every absence is explained
Attentiveness	Ten minutes to convene meeting, functions well afterward	Attention wanes after thirty minutes	Energy, attention high at beginning, decline by end of meeting	Members are alert and focused on the meeting or the task
Dependability	Tasks assigned	Tasks assigned and performed	Tasks volunteered for and usually performed	Tasks volunteered for and performed with enthusiasm

Five-Year Phasing Chart

Years / Strategic Directions	Year One	Year Two	Year Three	Year Four	Year Five

Three Stages Chart

Project: _____

Phase One: Preparation (Initiate, Mobilize, Adopt)	**Phase Two: Implementation** (Pilot)	**Phase Three: Continuation** (Incorporate, Institutionalize)

Balloon Master

Implementation Learnings Chart

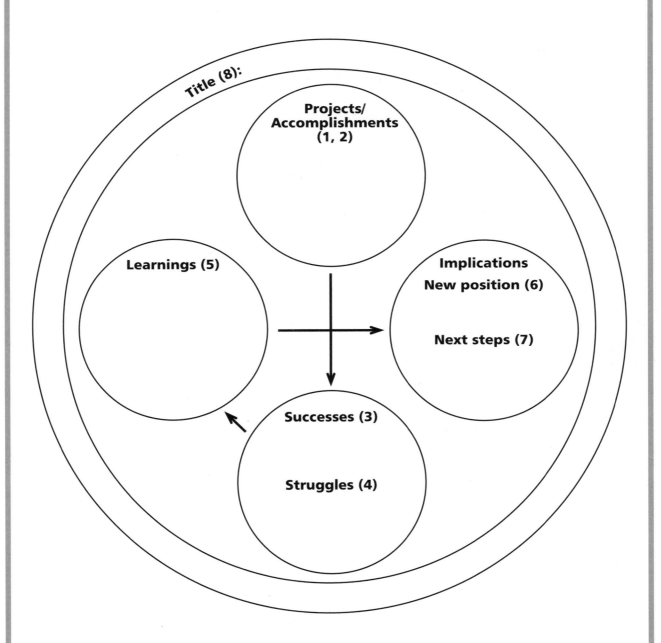

Title (8):

Projects/
Accomplishments
(1, 2)

Learnings (5)

Implications
New position (6)

Next steps (7)

Successes (3)

Struggles (4)

Resources Square

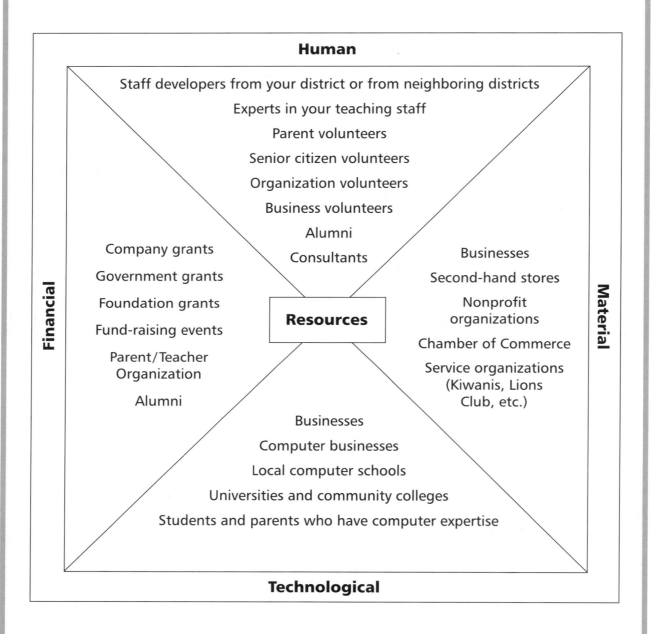

Human

Staff developers from your district or from neighboring districts

Experts in your teaching staff

Parent volunteers

Senior citizen volunteers

Organization volunteers

Business volunteers

Alumni

Consultants

Financial

Company grants

Government grants

Foundation grants

Fund-raising events

Parent/Teacher Organization

Alumni

Resources

Material

Businesses

Second-hand stores

Nonprofit organizations

Chamber of Commerce

Service organizations (Kiwanis, Lions Club, etc.)

Businesses

Computer businesses

Local computer schools

Universities and community colleges

Students and parents who have computer expertise

Technological

Source Location Chart

Needs	Potential Sources	Action Steps		
		What	When	Who

Community Resources Wheel

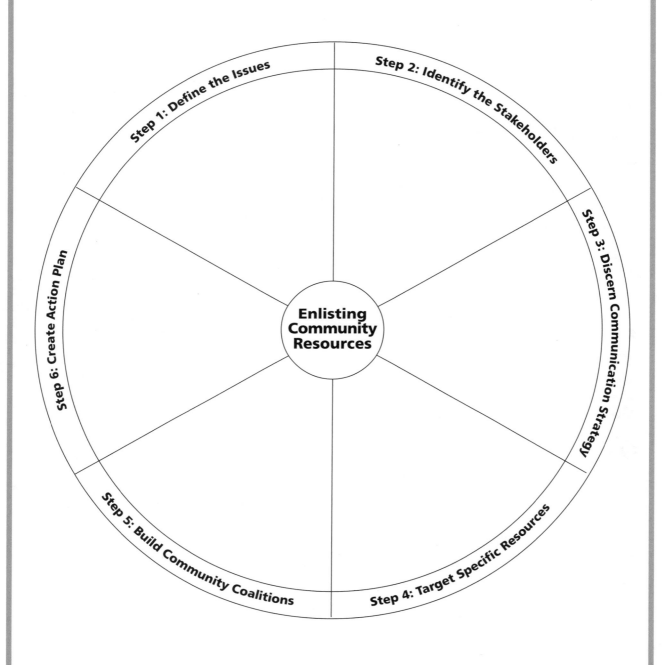

© 1997 IRI/SkyLight Training and Publishing, Inc.

Eventfulness Star

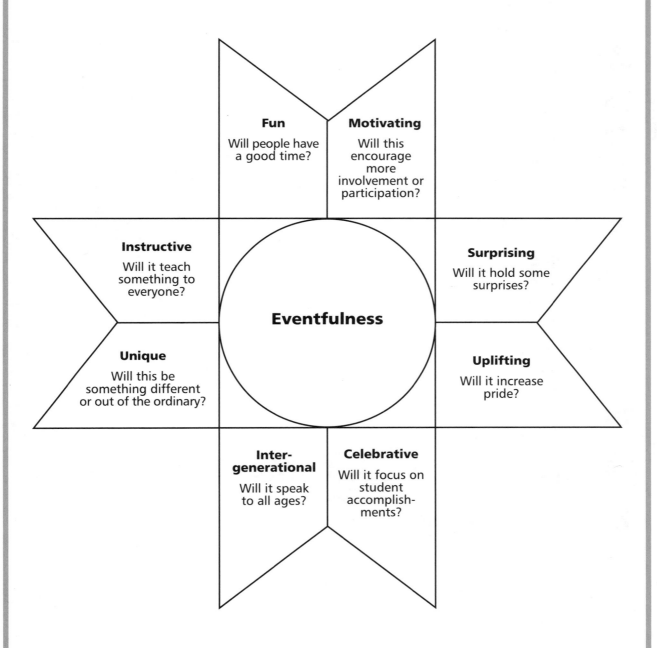

Fun
Will people have
a good time?

Motivating
Will this
encourage
more
involvement or
participation?

Instructive
Will it teach
something to
everyone?

Surprising
Will it hold some
surprises?

Eventfulness

Unique
Will this be
something different
or out of the ordinary?

Uplifting
Will it increase
pride?

**Inter-
generational**
Will it speak
to all ages?

Celebrative
Will it focus on
student
accomplish-
ments?

Getting the Media on Your Side

Keep the Focus on Learning Victories	Create a Dramatic and Informative Story	Plan Proactive Media Contact	Establish Personal Media Relationships	Expand Your Sphere of Influence

Adapted from Allan Holender, president of Educational Fundraising, Inc., Richmond, British Columbia.

Helpful Hints
for Media Contacts

- Don't expect your interview with the media to turn out the way you said it.

- Don't embellish your story. Just answer the question factually as presented and nothing more.

- Don't expect the media to be interested in everything you're doing.

- Don't be discouraged if they don't use what you gave them.

- Don't allow yourself to be interviewed unless you know what the specific questions will be.

- Don't be surprised if you are asked unexpected questions; expect the best, but prepare for the worst.

- Don't talk about other people; represent yourself only.

- Don't anger the media. They will come back to haunt you and haunt you and haunt you.

Adapted from Allan Holender, president of Educational Fundraising, Inc., Richmond, British Columbia.

Obstacle Reflection Wheel

How Obstacle Expresses Itself

What indicates that this obstacle is present? Who are most affected? How are they affected?

Solution Ideas

Quick fixes; Indirect or creative approaches; Direct or rational strategies; Long-term solutions

Information and Research Gathering

What happened? Who are the main actors? How many times has this occurred before? What does the research say about this obstacle and how to address it? How have other schools overcome this obstacle?

Apparent Obstacle

Systemic Obstacle

Working Toward Solutions

Who are potential allies? What elements of vision will be enhanced when the obstacle is dealt with? What are some possible aims?

Concrete vs. Illusory Venn Diagram

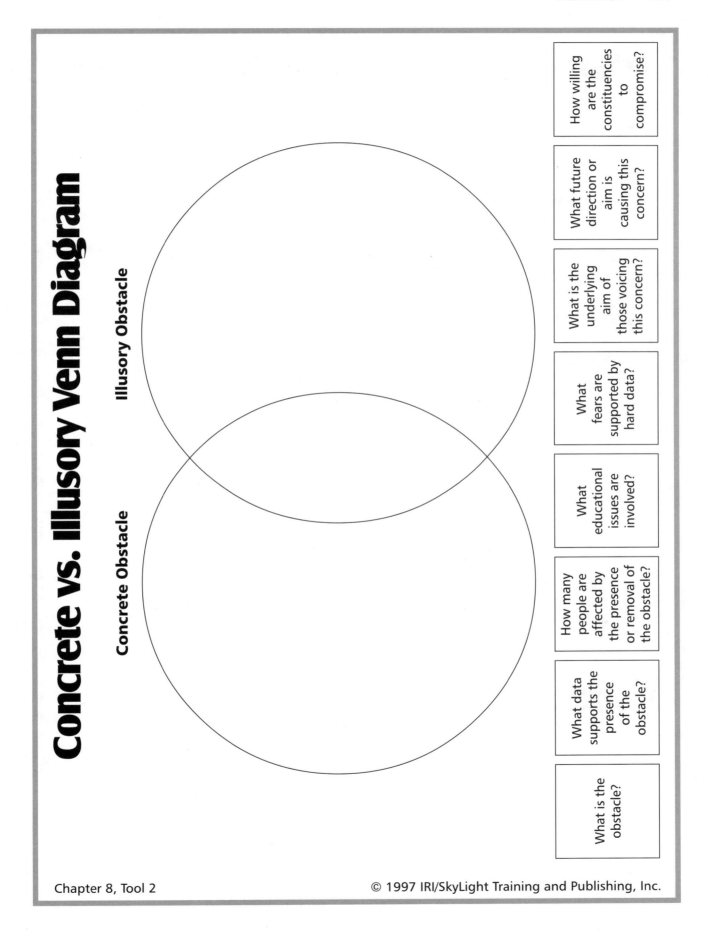

Concrete Obstacle

Illusory Obstacle

What is the obstacle?

What data supports the presence of the obstacle?

How many people are affected by the presence or removal of the obstacle?

What educational issues are involved?

What fears are supported by hard data?

What is the underlying aim of those voicing this concern?

What future direction or aim is causing this concern?

How willing are the constituencies to compromise?

Chapter 8, Tool 2

© 1997 IRI/SkyLight Training and Publishing, Inc.

Obstacles Analysis and Solution Matrix

		Obstacle 1	Obstacle 2	Obstacle 3	Cross-Obstacle Reflection
Analysis	**Name**				
	Symptoms				
	Structural/ Systemic Block				
Solutions	**Potential Allies**				
	Structural/ Systemic Solutions				
	Resources Needed				
	Next Steps				

Network Benefits Chart

Specific Network	Benefit(s) to Network	Benefit(s) to School

Reporting Format
for School-to-School Sharing

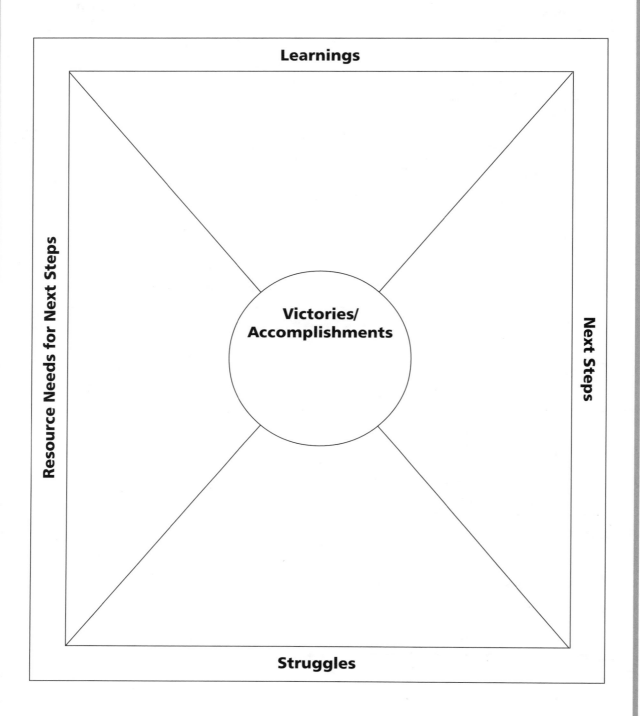

Learnings

Resource Needs for Next Steps

**Victories/
Accomplishments**

Next Steps

Struggles

Debriefing a Network on School Participation

Network:_____

1. What are some reports you heard from your employees?	
2. What did they like? What pleased them?	
3. What struggles did they enounter?	
4. How do your colleagues talk about how they have helped our school?	
5. How has this connection with our schools been a benefit for you?	
6. How could we improve this program next year?	

The Real Situation Chart

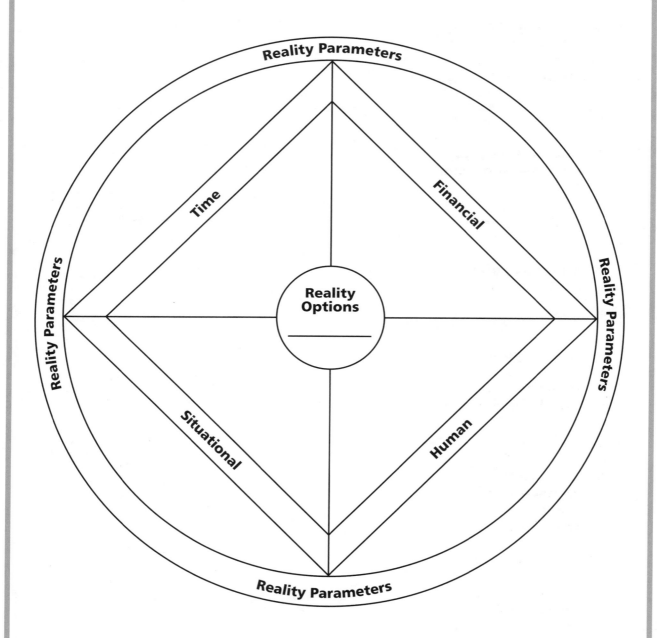

Why We Can't Go Back

Subject:

New Possibilities

**Why We Chose
the New**

**Why We Can't
Go Back**

Old Situation

"What's the Real Enemy?" Chart

**What happened?
What are the facts and details
behind the event?**

**How did we react to this
problem?**

**What would a
more helpful or
encouraging
structure or
system look like?**

**What steps can
we take to move
toward such a
structure?**

**What is the structural or
systemic enemy?**

**What are we really upset
or angry about?**

Energy Clues

Expressing Energy Activities	Inviting Quick Energy Activities
• The team has been engaged on a long-term project that hasn't produced any concrete or visible wins yet. • The team has many creative team members. • Teams have not gathered as a whole group for awhile.	• The team is usually perky but recently displays signs of decreasing energy. • The team has just been through one or two weeks of unusually hard work and team members are worn out. • The team has run into a small obstacle and team members feel they have had "the wind knocked out of them."
Honoring Energy Activities	**Generating Massive Energy Activities**
• The team feels certain that no one knows how hard they are working. • The team has been working for months and months without a celebration or recognition of its labors. • The team has produced a string of successes.	• The team has experienced a massive setback. • Many team members wonder why they signed up in the first place. • Members who have recently joined the team do not understand the big picture.

Human Structures/
Motivating Environment Screen

District

School

Teams

Data Gathering Questions

1. What facts, data, and other information are you noticing as you read and study this tool?

2. What connections and relationships are you discerning as you continue to study this tool?

3. What messages is this information communicating to us?

4. What is this telling us about what we are doing well? or What is this telling us about where our wins and victories are?

5. What are our next steps? What do we need to keep doing? What do we need to change?

Accomplishments Questionnaire

1. Name some of your projects or accomplishments from the past three months, six months, or year.

2. What projects or accomplishments have pleased or excited you the most?

3. How have these impacted your image of yourself as a teacher? What difference are these accomplishments making in your belief in the kind of teacher you are?

4. What are you ready to tackle now that maybe you weren't ready to tackle a year ago?

5. What's happening to us as an entire staff? How are we changing?

Our School Portfolio

Arena / Grade Level			

Create A Story Chart

Setting	Heroes/Heroines	Villains

Conflict	Resolution	Ending

Appendix B

Skills Context

Teacher training focuses on expanding the skills and teaching strategies of prospective facilitators. Both teachers and administrators are discovering the need to add facilitation skills to their repertoire of instructional and administrative skills.

Figure 1 represents the specific facilitation skills highlighted in this book. Figure 2 represents a list of facilitation skills compiled by a group getting trained in facilitation skills July 22–25, 1996, in Schaumburg, Illinois. The author thanks the participants for their work in putting this together and for their permission to use their compilation here.

The facilitator may use both charts to determine what skills are needed for effective facilitation.

Then he may analyze what skills he already possesses and what skills he may need to improve upon.

Finally, in addition to techniques and skills, there is the matter of the style of the facilitator. A facilitator may have the process and the techniques down perfectly; however, if the facilitator's style and personality do not communicate openness, trust, and confidence, getting the responses needed from other school change participants is difficult. An engaging style that projects accessibility helps ensure that the process is neither hindered nor brought to a standstill.

Skills for the Multidimensional Role of the Facilitator in School Change

Functions Elements	Process Leader	Skills Trainer	Resource Consultant	Group Energizer
Student Learning and Achievement	The Architect sees the big picture. • Enables the group to see the big picture • Expands the group's imagination • Uses skillful inquiry	The Coach devises strategies. • Uses a variety of teaching strategies • Employs the power of the team in instruction • Promotes processing	The Producer organizes the project. • Knows and relates to community • Implements events that spark interest and support • Uses flexible thinking	The Conductor stays true to the score. • Clarifies the real situation • Connects to original hopes and desires • Reveals options
Shared Decision-Making	The Carpenter builds consensus. • Fashions trust in the group • Honors the dignity of each person • Depends on the process	The Quarterback leads the team. • Passes on effective team processes • Involves everyone • Models collaboration	The Director overcomes obstacles. • Listens to the words behind words • Asks probing questions • Offers a variety of problem-solving tools	The Concertmaster harmonizes the environment. • Spreads power • Creates system-wide humanizing structures • Implements the fun and the unexpected
Visible Achievements	The Contractor steers the process. • Knows when to move to implementation • Enables the group to create marking points • Organizes the thinking	The Sportscaster announces the game. • Shares information • Moves the group to more complex victories • Reports on victories	The Promoter advertises successes. • Links needs together • Connects with people positively • Makes surprising connections	The Critic Celebrates the performance. • Pays close attention to the performance • Interprets information • Tells powerful stories

Figure 1

IRI/SkyLight Training and Publishing, Inc.

What Are the Skills of an Effective Facilitator?

Directing the Group's Energy	Enouraging the Affective	Implementing the Process	Using Clear and Insightful Communication	Caring for the Individual	Modeling a Professional, Proactive, Collaborative Attitude	Creating a Fun, Enthusiastic Event
Keeps goals in mind

Continually focuses on the big picture | Senses group's needs: mood, climate

Inspires passion

Honors everyone's dignity

Reads people

Practices patience

Expresses positive outlook and demeanor | Manipulates action

Knows and honors the process

Understands the process roles and strategies

Maintains objectivity

Manages process and agenda

Focuses on tasks

Sits on own opinions

Remains neutral | Paraphrases

Synthesizes information

Listen for the words behind the words

Summarizes statements

Communicates verbally

Effective questioning techniques

Thinks well on feet

Probes to get specific responses

Reads the group | Dignifies the responses

Exemplifies tact and courtesy

Honors group and individuals

Seeks first to understand

Caretaker of participant's feelings

Realizes importance of each individual as well as importance of group

Stays open to all points of view

Affirms contributions | Works with a sense of stewardship

Does not judge or rebuke

Models organization

Responds with flexibility

Facilitates instead of dominates

Fosters professional attitudes

Thinks in terms of win-win | Exhibits enthusiasm and dedication

Uses a sense of humor

Cares for the space

Practices creative approaches |

Figure 2

IRI/SkyLight Training and Publishing, Inc.

Bibliography

Astuto, T. A., D. L. Clark, A. M. Read, K. McGree, and L. DeKoven Pelton Fernandez. 1994. *Roots of reform: Challenging the assumptions that control change in education.* Bloomington, Ind.: Phi Delta Kappa Educational Foundation.

Bellanca, J. and R. Fogarty. 1991. *Blueprints for thinking in the cooperative classroom.* Arlington Heights, Ill.: IRI/SkyLight Training and Publishing.

Bennett, B. and C. Rolheiser-Bennett. 1992. A restructuring journey. In A. Costa, J. Bellanca, and R. Fogarty, eds. 1992. *If minds matter: A foreward to the future. Vols I & II.* Arlington Heights, Ill.: IRI/SkyLight Training and Publishing.

Blythe, T. and H. Gardner. 1990. A school for all intelligences. *Educational Leadership* 47(7): 33–37.

Bolman, L. G. and T. E. Deal. 1995. *Leading with soul.* San Francisco: Jossey-Bass.

Boyer, E. 1994. A vision for community education. *Edges* 6(2): 29–32.

Brassard, M. and D. Ritter. 1994. *The Memory Jogger.* Methuen, Mass.: Goal/QPC.

Burke, K. 1994. *The mindful school: How to assess authentic learning.* Arlington Heights, Ill.: IRI/SkyLight Training and Publishing.

Burke, K., R. Fogarty, and S. Belgrad. 1994. *The mindful school: The portfolio connection.* Arlington Heights, Ill.: IRI/SkyLight Training and Publishing.

Byham, W. C. 1992. *Zapp! in education.* New York: Fawcett Columbine.

Chapman, C. 1993. *If the shoe fits . . . . : How to develop multiple intelligences in the classroom.* Arlington Heights, Ill.: IRI/SkyLight Training and Publishing.

Costa, A., J. Bellanca, and R. Fogarty, eds. 1992. *If minds matter: A foreword to the future. Vols I & II.* Arlington Heights, Ill.: IRI/SkyLight Training and Publishing.

Covey, S. R. 1990. *The 7 habits of highly effective people: Powerful lessons in personal change.* New York: Simon & Schuster.

Daniels, C. T. 1990. A principal's view: Giving up my traditional ship. *The School Administrator* 47(8): 20–24.

David, J. L. 1991. What it takes to restructure education. *Educational Leadership* 48(8): 11–15.

Deal, T. E. 1990. Reframing reform. *Educational Leadership* 47(8): 6–12.

Doyle, D. P. and S. Pimentel. 1993. A study in change: Transforming the Charlotte-Mecklenburg Schools. *Phi Delta Kappan* 74(7): 534–539.

Ellis, S. S. 1994. Everyone is a leader in a "School for the 21st Century": A profile of Susan Derse. *Journal of Staff Development* 15(4): 58–59.

Fogarty, R. 1995. *Best practices for the learner-centered classroom.* Arlington Heights, Ill.: IRI/SkyLight Training and Publishing.

Foster, K. 1990. Small steps on the way to teacher empowerment. *Educational Leadership* 47(8): 38–40.

Fullan, M. G. 1994. Masks of the teacher. *Edges* 6(2): 14–18.

Fullan, M. G. with S. Stiegelbauer. 1991. *The new meaning of educational change.* New York: Teachers College Press.

Gallegos, J. L. 1994. Staff development strategies that facilitate a transition in educational paradigms. *Journal of Staff Development* 15(4): 34–38.

Gardner, H. 1983. *Frames of mind: The theory of multiple intelligences.* New York: HarperCollins.

Gardner, H. 1996. Your child's intelligence(s). *Scholastic Parent and Child* 3(3): 32–37.

Glasser, W. 1990. *The quality school.* New York: Harper & Row Perennial Library.

Glickman, C. 1991. Pretending not to know what we know. *Educational Leadership* 48(8): 4–10.

Goldman, C. and C. O'Shea. 1990. A culture for change. *Educational Leadership* 47(8): 41–43.

Goodlad, J. I. 1994. The national network for educational renewal. *Phi Delta Kappan* 75(8): 632–638.

Holmes, D. 1996. Facilitating social change. *Edges: New Planetary Patterns.* 7(3): 2–4.

Honig, B. 1991. *Recipes for creative teamwork.* San Anselmo, Calif.: Bruce Honig and Associates.

Ingwerson, D. W. 1990. A superintendent's view: Learning to listen and trust each school faculty. *The School Administrator* 47(8): 8–11.

Johnston, J. A., W. E. Bickel, and R. C. Wallace, Jr. 1990. Building and sustaining change in the culture of secondary schools. *Educational Leadership* 47(8): 46–48.

Joyce, B. and B. Showers. 1988. *Student achievement through staff development.* New York: Longman.

Joyce, B., J. Wolf, and E. Calhoun. 1993. *The self-renewing school.* Alexandria, Va.: Association for Supervision and Curriculum Development.

Lieberman, A. 1988. Expanding the leadership team. *Educational Leadership* 45(5): 4–8.

Maeroff, G. I. 1993. Building teams to rebuild schools. *Phi Delta Kappan* 74(7): 512–519.

Miles, M. B. and K. S. Louis. 1990. Mustering the will and skill for change. *Educational Leadership* 47(8): 57–61.

Moffett, J. 1994. On to the past: Wrong-headed school reform. *Phi Delta Kappan* 75(8): 584–590.

Morgan, G. 1986. *Images of organization.* Newbury Park, Calif.: SAGE Publications.

National Education Commission on Time and Learning. Prisoners of time. A report from the National Education Commission on Time and Learning. Washington, D.C.: U.S. Department of Education.

Peters, T. 1987. *Thriving on chaos.* New York: Alfred A. Knopf.

Rubin, B. M. 1995. Jumping off the fast track. *Chicago Tribune Magazine,* January 22, 10–15.

Russell, W. *Preparing collaborative leaders: A facilitator's guide.* Washington, D.C.: Institute for Educational Leadership.

Saxl, E., M. Miles, and A. Lieberman. 1990. *Assisting change in education (ACE).* Alexandria, Va.: Association for Supervision and Curriculum Development.

Scearce, C. 1992. *100 ways to build teams.* Arlington Heights, Ill.: IRI/SkyLight Training and Publishing.

Schrenko, L. 1994. *Structuring a learner-centered school.* Arlington Heights, Ill.: IRI/SkyLight Training and Publishing.

Seif, E. 1990. How to create schools that thrive in chaotic times. *Educational Leadership* 47(8): 81–82.

Sergiovanni, T. J. 1992. *Moral leadership: Getting to the heart of school improvement.* San Francisco: Jossey-Bass.

Simpson, G. W. 1990. Keeping it alive: Elements of school culture that sustain innovation. *Educational Leadership* 47(8): 34–37.

Sizer, T. R. 1991. No pain, no gain. *Educational Leadership* 48(8): 32–34.

Slavin, R. E. 1991. Synthesis of research on cooperative learning. *Educational Leadership* 48(5): 71–82.

Spencer, L. J. 1989. *Winning through participation.* Dubuque, Iowa: Kendall/Hunt.

Troxel, J. P., ed. 1993. *Participation works: Business cases from around the world.* Alexandria, Va.: Miles River Press.

Wheatley, M. J. 1992. *Leadership and the new science.* San Francisco, Calif.: Berrett-Koehler.

Williams, R. B. 1996. Four dimensions of the school change facilitator. *Journal of Staff Development* 17(1): 48–50.

Williams, R. B. 1993. *More than 50 ways to build team consensus.* Arlington Heights, Ill.: IRI/SkyLight Training and Publishing.

Index

There are
one-story intellects,
two-story intellects, and three-story
intellects with skylights. All fact collectors, who
have no aim beyond their facts, are one-story men. Two-story men
compare, reason, generalize, using the labors of the fact collectors as
well as their own. Three-story men idealize, imagine,
predict—their best illumination comes from
above, through the skylight.
—*Oliver Wendell*
Holmes

SkyLight

PROFESSIONAL DEVELOPMENT

We Prepare Your Teachers Today
for the Classrooms of Tomorrow

Learn from Our Books and from Our Authors!

Ignite Learning in Your School or District.

SkyLight's team of classroom-experienced consultants can help you foster systemic change for increased student achievement.

Professional development is a process not an event. SkyLight's experienced practitioners drive the creation of our on-site professional development programs, graduate courses, research-based publications, interactive video courses, teacher-friendly training materials, and online resources—call SkyLight Professional Development today.

SkyLight specializes in three professional development areas.

Specialty #  **1**

Best Practices

We **model** the best practices that result in improved student performance and guided applications.

Specialty #  **2**

Making the Innovations Last

We help set up **support** systems that make innovations part of everyday practice in the long-term systemic improvement of your school or district.

Specialty #  **3**

How to Assess the Results

We prepare your school leaders to encourage and **assess** teacher growth, **measure** student achievement, and **evaluate** program success.

Contact the SkyLight team and begin a process toward long-term results.

SkyLight Professional Development

2626 S. Clearbrook Dr., Arlington Heights, IL 60005
800-348-4474 • 847-290-6600 • FAX 847-290-6609
info@skylightedu.com • www.skylightedu.com